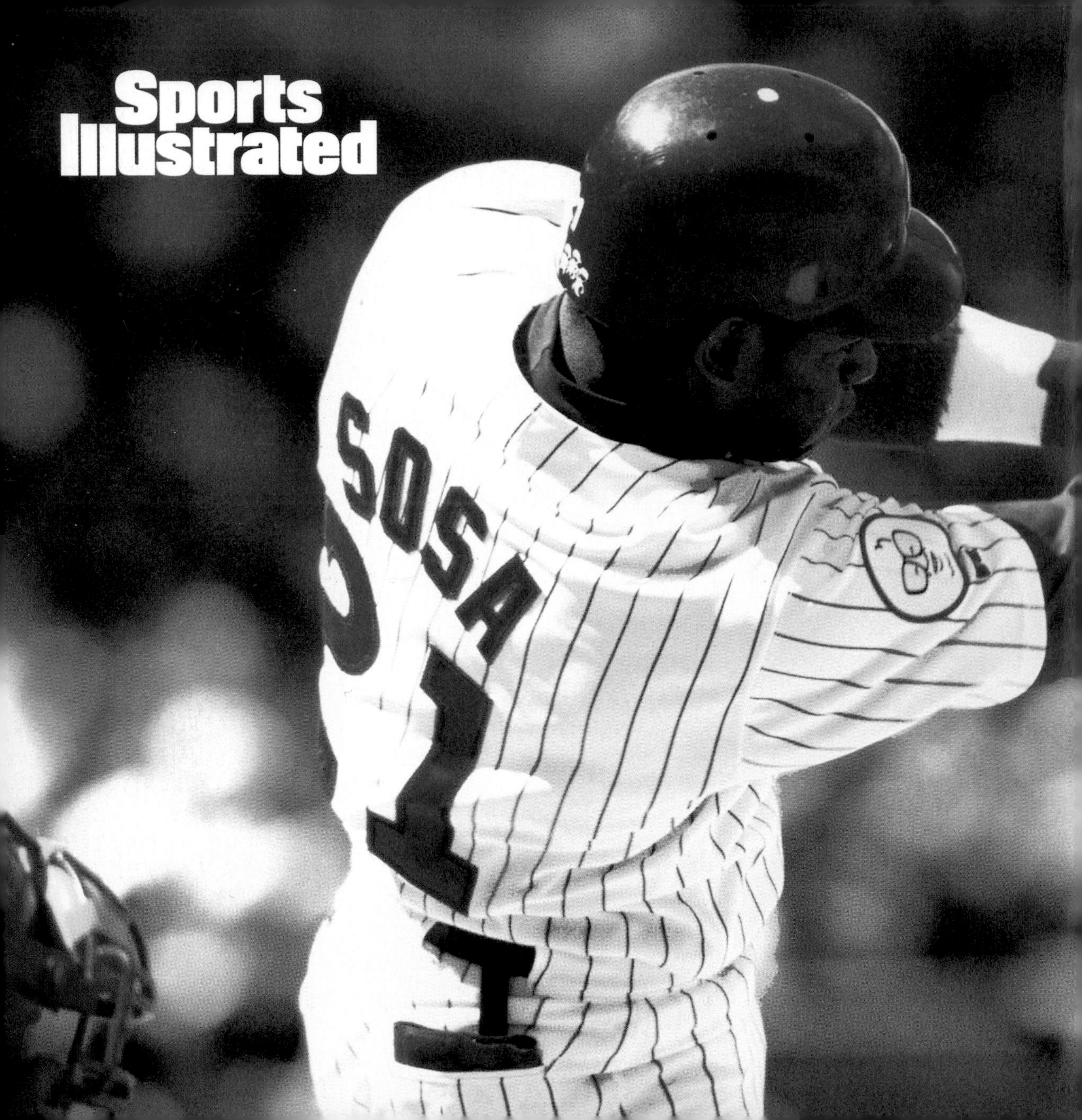
Sports Illustrated
SOSA

Home Run Heroes
Mark McGwire, Sammy Sosa, and a Season for the Ages

Stories excerpted from the pages of *Sports Illustrated*
Original text by Merrell Noden

SIMON & SCHUSTER

Simon & Schuster
Rockefeller Center
1230 Avenue of the Americas
New York, NY 10020

SIMON & SCHUSTER and colophon are registered trademarks of Simon & Schuster Inc.
SPORTS ILLUSTRATED is a registered trademark of Time Inc.

Home Run Heroes: Mark McGwire, Sammy Sosa, and a Season for the Ages was produced by Bishop
Books Inc., New York City.

Manufactured in the United States of America

10 9 8 7 6 5 4 3 2 1

Library of Congress Cataloging-in-Publication Data is available.

ISBN: 0-684-86357-X

Contents

Introduction

By Merrell Noden

There is something literally uplifting about the sight of a baseball streaking across the sky and disappearing over an outfield fence. It lifts people from their seats, turns upward the faces of fans and players alike and leaves them transfixed, like true believers awaiting the performance of a miracle.

In the astonishing season just past, a season in which an entire new math of gaudy statistics could not do justice to the flesh-and-blood excitement of it all, baseball was at its uplifting best. Entire stadiums came to resemble scenes from *Close Encounters of the Third Kind,* Steven Spielberg's fuzzy fable of intergalactic brotherhood. In ballpark after ballpark, all around the country, thousands stood, turned rapt faces to the skies and then exploded in cheers at the sight of Mark McGwire of the St. Louis Cardinals and Sammy Sosa of the Chicago Cubs launching baseballs into space, racing each other towards one of the game's most hallowed records: Roger Maris's single-season home run record of 61. It was one of the rare times when an entire nation was bound together by a single, joyous pursuit. You couldn't have escaped it even if you'd wanted to, though of course no one did.

And while it was an extraordinary season all around—the Yankees won an American League record 114 games, Cal Ripken benched himself to halt his streak of consecutive-games-played at a Methuselahian 2,632 games, and the San Francisco Giants, the New York Mets and Sosa's Cubs battled for the National League wild-card playoff spot right up to the final game of the season—it was the home run race that juiced us all. "Goin' Yard" became the slang term of choice to describe the act of hitting a home run. It was perfect, conjuring up adult power on one hand and sweet childhood memories of backyard ballgames on the other. Who among us doesn't recall the thrill of smashing one over the fence and then waiting, cringing, for the sound of a breaking window? Sosa, in fact, broke countless windshields on Waveland Avenue, just over the leftfield bleachers in

Although he tired of the media's incessant demands, McGwire always had time for the fans.

Wrigley Field. But in baseball-mad Wrigleyville, festooned with Dominican flags, nobody seemed to mind.

Somewhere along the way, Sosa cracked—in the immortal words of *Saturday Night Live* character Chico Escuela—that baseball had been "berry, berry good" to him, and while that's undoubtedly true, he and McGwire paid the game back with interest. Three years after a strike forced the first-ever cancellation of the World Series, baseball desperately needed this record chase. So, it seemed, did we all. A record 70,589,505 fans attended games, with McGwire's Cards and Sosa's Cubbies drawing the most fans on the road.

What made the whole experience sweeter was the class demonstrated by these two very different men. Again and again Sosa pronounced McGwire "The Man," and if those professions of admiration were really just a shrewd way of deflecting the spotlight, it sure didn't seem like it. These two guys genuinely liked each other. To fans grown tired of selfish, trash-talking millionaires, their gentlemanly, good-humored respect for one another—their surpassing grace in the face of extraordinary pressure—reminded us how inspiring true sportsmanship can be. If McGwire seemed to be having something less than a good time for a few weeks in August, it served to make him a little more like us, and we forgave him. Even Big Mac, that Bunyanesque smasher of tape measure home runs, was human.

Home-run fever had many symptoms, but delirium was the most pronounced. The only sight more familiar than McGwire or Sosa circling the bases was that of grown men and women, accountants, lawyers and teachers, diving recklessly for home run balls. The slug fest became a hug fest. "There was only one thing we wanted from him," said the wife of the man who caught McGwire's 66th. "That was a hug." Well, get in line: Interviewing McGwire after his record-setting blast, Fox broadcaster Jack Buck began by asking for ... a hug.

Yet our late summer madness made perfect sense. What a lousy year it would have been without McGwire and Sosa! Hardly a day went by without more upsetting proof that the Real World was spinning crazily off its axis: The terrorist bombing of U.S. embassies in Nairobi and Dar es Salaam, the mysterious crash of a Swissair jet, the collapse of markets from Brazil to Russia and the Far East, and worst of all, the excruciatingly embarrassing details of the Clinton-Lewinsky affair. The spectacle of McGwire chasing Maris and Sosa chasing McGwire was a delicious respite from all that. Whereas broadcasters had to warn children away from the room before reciting the details of the Starr report, the home-run race was 100% kid-friendly, the stuff of childhood dreams. Thanks to baseball, what might have been the worst of times became the best of times, a giddy, breathless march towards history.

9

As fan-friendly as McGwire, Sosa tossed a souvenir into the rightfield bleachers before a game at Wrigley.

Chasing History

Chasing History

By Merrell Noden

Before it was his, the great slugger Hank Aaron described the career home record as the "Cadillac" of all baseball records. Though one hates to disagree with the most prolific of all home run hitters—especially when one recalls the death threats he received when it became clear he would break Babe Ruth's career mark of 714 homers—Aaron was wrong.

Granted, the career record is proof of superhuman consistency. Aaron's 755 home runs average out to 19 seasons of nearly 40 home runs each, a truly staggering feat. But it is the single-season mark that generates the most excitement, largely because a single season, 162 games running from greenest spring through the dog days of summer and on into the cool fall nights, is a stretch of time around which we can all wrap our imaginations. A season is long enough for anticipation to build, for front runners to fade and dark horses to emerge, yet not so long that it can't sustain our interest. There is poetry in the very idea of The Season: Whereas a career is a kind of human construct, a season is natural, part of the earth's rhythm.

For most of the 37 seasons that had passed since Roger Maris set the single-season record of 61 home runs, no one even scared that record. Willie Mays hit 52 homers in 1965, George Foster matched that in '77 and Cecil Fielder hit 51 in '90—but 51 is still 10 homers shy of tying Maris. Recalling the media pressure, the incessant, repetitive questioning, that awaited anyone who approached even 50, it seemed as if Maris's record had acquired its own protective armor. Reggie Jackson had 37 homers at the All-Star break in 1969; he ended the season with 47.

No one knew better than Maris the perils of challenging the record. An intensely private man who resented the popular affection reserved for Ruth and for his own, more beloved teammate, Mickey Mantle, Maris suffered terribly throughout that historic season. His hair fell out and he became a prisoner of his hotel room. "Nobody knows how tired I am," he said. The final indignity was seeing an asterisk next to his name in the record book, as if somehow he were responsible for adding eight games to the 154-game schedule Ruth had played. That was the price to be paid for daring to challenge an American legend like Ruth.

With 52 home runs in '96 and 58 in '97, McGwire seemed to have the best shot at Maris in '98.

tics, skewing them upwards. Nineteen sixty-one was an expansion year, and so was 1977, when Foster hit his 52. If the record was going to go, observers thought, 1998 might well be the season.

McGwire seemed to have the best shot at it. At 6' 5", 250 pounds, with 19" biceps, he takes as big and vicious a cut as anyone in the game. Anytime he hits the ball in the air, it stands a good chance of leaving the park, as proven by the fact that he opened the season second only to Ruth in career home-run efficiency, having hit one out every 11.94 at bats. What's more, McGwire had just notched back-to-back 50-homer seasons, a feat only he and the Babe had ever accomplished.

There were a number of players who seemed capable of pushing McGwire—Belle, Frank Thomas, Mike Piazza, Juan Gonzalez and any number of the residents of mile high Coors Field—but his main rival seemed to be Griffey, the Seattle Mariners' great centerfielder, a veteran of nine big league seasons at age 28. Relying on a seemingly effortless "flick" of a swing, Griffey had smashed 56 home runs in the 1997 season and was on pace to eventually surpass the career mark of Aaron (who, incidentally, never topped 50 in a single season).

So McGwire, it seemed, would have company. When he tied a Willie Mays record by homering in the first four games of the season, it looked as if April would indeed be the cruelest month—for pitchers, that is. By the end of April, Big Mac had racked up 11, and this most memorable of seasons was underway.

But suddenly, starting in 1995, Maris's mark began to look very breakable. Albert Belle hit 50 that year, while Mark McGwire and shocking Brady Anderson cracked 52 and 50, respectively, in '96, a season which set the major league record for home run frequency. By 1997, when McGwire hit 58 and Ken Griffey Jr. 56, we seemed to have entered a new Golden Age of home run slugging.

And there was further cause for excitement in 1998. Two new franchises were entering the major leagues—the Tampa Bay Devil Rays and the Arizona Diamondbacks—and expansion almost always magnifies great players' statis-

Man on a Mission

Tom Verducci's profile of Mark McGwire in SI's baseball preview issue reported on the slugger's highly anticipated assault on Roger Maris's home run record; it also revealed the softer side of McGwire, a man who cries every once in a while, bleeds for the plight of abused children, and is determined to be the best father he possibly can to his 10-year-old son.

By Tom Verducci

At the very same spot every winter's day, as he returns home from his weight-training session, Mark McGwire eases up a bit on the gas pedal of one of only 172 special-edition Porsches in the world. McGwire is such a large man that he seems to be not so much driving the silver sports car as wearing it—a suit of armor with cruise control. He is so big that his forearms are the same circumference as the neck of a very large man: 17½ inches. The steering wheel is a doughnut in his massive hands.

The sight that prompts his caution is so unremarkable as to be ignored by most everyone else driving in this quiet Orange County, Calif., neighborhood. Beyond a chain-link fence is an ordinary elementary school with grassy ball fields, a blacktop basketball court and, of course, children. It could be any school in any town, and that's exactly what worries McGwire. As the Porsche slows, this is what he imagines on the other side of the fence: frightened souls and shattered lives.

"What kills me is that you know there are kids over there who are being abused or neglected, you just don't know which ones," McGwire says.

"And most of the adults who are doing it get away with it. It just breaks my heart."

Statistics on child abuse are tricky and, because many cases go unreported, a little like trying to count fish in the ocean. Two widely cited studies of sexual abuse in the U.S. and Canada estimate that one of every three girls is abused before her 18th birthday and that one in six boys is abused before he turns 16. (Other studies cite different percentages.) A simple kickball game becomes an achingly sad math problem. How many children are there? Maybe 30. How many will know the horror? Seven, maybe eight. Who are they? And why does the most amazing home run hitter since Babe Ruth cry for them?

The biggest, strongest man in baseball is really a softy. His eyesight is 20/500, which means that without his contacts, he is Mr. Magoo. His glasses have lenses that could have been pilfered from the Hubble telescope. His body breaks down more than a '76 Pinto. He has such an awkward, knock-kneed batting style that he had barely buttoned up a professional uniform when

La Russa's prediction that McGwire "might hit 70" seemed exaggerated—in the preseason.

a coach in the Oakland organization told him, "You'll never hit in the major leagues like *that*." He has seen a therapist. He's unlucky at love. He thinks the man who married his ex-wife, Kathy, is a terrific guy. He aches to see more of his 10-year-old son, Matthew. And if the next time you go to the movies you happen to see a great big redhead crying in a nearby seat, that could be the guy who has hit more homers in one season than any man alive. "Oh, sure, I cry at some of them," says McGwire, the first baseman for the St. Louis Cardinals. "I mean, how can you not cry watching *Philadelphia*? And *Driving Miss Daisy*? I cried at that."

This giant is more sensitive than a sunburn, though pitchers might have a difficult time believing that. "The one creepy thought I have when he comes up there," says righthander Curt Schilling of the Philadelphia Phillies, "is the fear that he'll hit my best pitch right back up the middle. He's the one guy in baseball who could hit a ball that goes in one side of you and out the other, and it would be going just as fast when it came out."

McGwire hits home runs so far that you can measure them with your car; he launched one off Randy Johnson last year that would have clicked off more than one tenth of a mile on the odometer. He hits them so often (one every 11.9 at bats in his career) that he is nearing Ruth's career-record frequency (11.8), thanks to an astounding run over the last three years (8.6) that is unprecedented in baseball history.

Everything about him is big: 6'5", 250 pounds, 20-inch biceps, 538-foot home runs and 58 dingers, his total last season—the closest anyone has come to the sport's sexiest record in the 37 years since Roger Maris hit 61, a record never more endangered than it is right now.

"Mark is one of those players who is so special, you cannot put limits on what he can do," says Cardinals manager Tony La Russa. "He might hit 40, 50 or 60 this year. He might hit 70."

McGwire came up just short of the record last year despite hitting only three home runs while in a 33-day fog—the period during which he endured daily trade rumors and ultimately, with a July 31 swap between the Oakland A's and St. Louis, a switch in leagues. Now only the Arch is more of a fixture in St. Louis than a contented McGwire, who is 34. As was the case for Maris in '61, this season will be a fascinating convergence of an expansion year, with its inevitable dilution of major league pitching talent, and a career that seems to be peaking.

"I've always appreciated how difficult it is," McGwire says of hitting 61, "and now I know how possible it is. I hit 58 and had a terrible July. But it would have to be almost a perfect season for it to happen."

How will it add up? Never have there been better reasons for marking McGwire. Yet the numbers he prefers to talk about are the ones that refer to children he's never met. That, too, is the measurement of McGwire.

He pulls the Porsche into his garage, with its black-and-gray rubberized floor so spotlessly shiny that you think, for a moment, that he might have parked in the wrong spot—perhaps the gourmet kitchen. "I'm kind of a neat freak," he says, unnecessarily.

There is almost no evidence that a ballplayer lives in this tastefully decorated harborside house. McGwire gave his 1990 Gold Glove to his optometrist to display in his office. He gave one of his two Silver Slugger bats to his father, John, a dentist, to hang in his office. Like most of his other trophies and mementos, his 1987 Rookie of the Year Award is stashed in a storage facility. McGwire exudes a remarkable lack of self-importance for someone in the look-at-me culture of pro sports. For instance, the gym he frequents is a busy but ordinary family fitness center tucked in a strip mall. Mothers in spandex lug their toddlers to the baby sitting room, and off-duty policemen and firemen want to know the secret for developing forearms like his. "Genetics," he tells them. "You should see my father."

John McGwire provided his son with inspiration, not just genes. At seven John was bedridden for months with an illness that left him with one leg much shorter than the other. But John was interested in all sorts of sports, eventually training as an amateur boxer. One of Mark's earliest memories is the rat-a-tat-tat of a speed bag echoing in the garage as John pounded away.

His father's influence has never waned. One night in Oakland a few years back, John happened to be following Mark out of the players' lot when someone in a BMW raced in front of McGwire, cutting him off. "Mark! Mark!" the driver yelled. "You have to sign this for my son. You're his hero! Please! You're his hero!"

The turmoil of his departure from the A's may have kept McGwire from reaching Maris's record in '97.

McGwire jumped out of his car and marched over to the man. "You, sir, as a parent, should be your son's hero," he said, pointing his finger. "Not me!" Then he signed a baseball card.

No matter where you sit or stand in Mark McGwire's house, it is impossible not to have within sight a framed picture of his son. On the last day of the 1987 season, needing one home run for 50, McGwire excused himself to be by his wife's side when Matthew was born. (He and Kathy were married too young, he says, and were divorced a year later.) "I was born on October 1, and he was born on October 4. It's scary how much alike we are. I don't have to say a word to him sometimes, because he knows what I'm thinking."

Mark grew up happily in the Los Angeles suburb

of Claremont, Calif., with four brothers. About the worst thing that happened to him was walking so many batters while pitching in a Little League game that he cried right there on the mound. His father, a coach, told him to switch places with the shortstop. But even that came with a silver lining. "I can still remember looking in at the plate from shortstop, and everything was real fuzzy," McGwire says. "I got glasses right after that."

It was only in the past two years that the issue of child abuse touched a nerve. Two friends told him that they had been abused as children; then he began dating a woman who worked at a home that assists sexually abused children. He met some of the kids and began to learn about the numbers. One morning he stood in the doorway of the home as parents dropped off their children for therapy. How could you? he thought.

"It's a calling," he says. "I'm a firm believer that children can't recognize what is happening to them, and they cannot be the adults they want to be unless they can get help. The biggest thing I'm trying to do is make sure the money goes to the right place. I want every dollar to help the children."

McGwire refuses to participate in events where people are charged for his autograph—unless the money goes to charity. As part of a three-day benefit for Cardinals Care, a charitable foundation set up by the ball club, he had agreed to sign for 300 people. Half the tickets to be redeemed for his signature at Monday's session would be sold on Saturday and half on Sunday. When the benefit began at a downtown St. Louis hotel, a stampede

like nothing seen this side of Pamplona took dead aim on the McGwire ticket booth. La Russa quickly telephoned McGwire to ask a favor.

"I know you said 300, but could you sign more?" he asked.

"How many?" McGwire said.

"How about 400?"

"Let's make it 500."

For three solid hours on Monday, McGwire signed for a procession of fans. Listening to them during their 20 seconds with McGwire, you would not have been surprised if some of them were carrying gold, frankincense and myrrh.

"I know the home runs come first, but a lot of people are going to remember you for your generosity."

"Thank you for staying in St. Louis, Mark."

"I work with abused children, and I just want to thank you for what you're doing."

The next night McGwire is seated at the dais at the St. Louis baseball writers' dinner when he gets up to use the rest room. Many in the crowd push away from their tables, too. McGwire enters the rest room, slips into a stall. When he is done, he opens the stall door and can't believe his eyes: The room is packed shoulder to shoulder with men all pretending to have heard nature's call at the same moment.

"I've never seen or heard about St. Louis falling for a player like they've done for this guy," said Brian Bartow, the Cardinals director of media relations, who's been with the team since 1987. "Not for Musial, not for Gibson, not for Ozzie—nobody."

18

Soon after McGwire arrived in St. Louis, NL pitchers learned to fear his awesome power at the plate.

The National League had not seen a 50-home-run hitter since Cincinnati's George Foster hit 52 in 1977. McGwire became St. Louis's traveling exhibit. In Chicago fans jammed Waveland Avenue outside Wrigley Field as McGwire's batting-practice shots fell like hailstones in September. In Denver, McGwire hit a ball out of Coors Field and into the players' parking lot.

McGwire's appeal in St. Louis, though, is even more powerful than that. He made baseball fans feel as if they mattered again. "With the A's, I lived downtown in San Francisco last year for the first time," says McGwire, who had resided in suburban Alamo. "The city is so full of life, so many things to do. I felt so much energy living there. But when I left for the ballpark, by the time I was halfway over the Bay Bridge, there was no more energy. Then I came to St. Louis, and the people just overwhelmed me. I had never felt anything like that. The energy level was incredible."

There is an undeniable element of novelty to McGwire's appeal. Two generations of fans have grown up in St. Louis without seeing a premier power hitter in their hometown. Only three men have hit more than 35 home runs in a season for the Cardinals—Rogers Hornsby, Johnny Mize and Stan Musial—none since 1949. In the second half of last season Cardinals fans were so eager to watch McGwire take a few hacks, even against out-of-shape coaches, that the club opened the Busch Stadium gates and concessions two hours before game time for batting practice, a policy that will continue this year.

Five weeks after the trade, McGwire called up his attorney, Robert Cohen, and said, "I want to stay here. Let's see if we can work out a deal with the Cardinals." A flabbergasted Cohen told McGwire to get a good night's sleep—and reconsider. McGwire was only two months away from being the focus of a free-agent bidding war. The Anaheim Angels, who had been rumored to be pursuing McGwire, showed no interest in bringing him home to be near Matthew. But surely large-market teams would create another huge McGwire number, one with a dollar sign preceding it. "Don't be surprised to hear from the Braves," Cohen said. When McGwire woke

19

up the next day, he hadn't changed his mind.

Ten days later McGwire agreed to a three-year contract extension that guarantees him $30 million and will add another $9 million if a mutual option for a fourth year is exercised. He also pulls in $1 for every ticket sold beyond 2.8 million. (The Cards averaged 2.64 million over the previous two years.) And Matthew gets a seat on the team plane when he visits Dad during the summer. "Sure, I could have gotten more money, but why?" McGwire says. "I had everything that I wanted right in St. Louis."

On Sept. 16, 1997, at the press conference to announce his new deal, McGwire said he was establishing a foundation to dispense $1 million a year for at least the next three years to help abused and neglected children. When a reporter asked a question about his concern for abused children, something strange happened to McGwire. He thought about all the kids in the world—kids the same age as Matthew—who have had the blessing of childhood ripped away from them. His mouth opened, but all he could do was cry. The cameras kept rolling, and 33 seconds passed before he could speak again.

"I surprised myself," McGwire says. "I didn't know all that emotion was going to come out."

In '91 McGwire hit 22 home runs, drove in 75 runs—and didn't ask for a raise. That year he also hit .201, quit lifting weights out of sheer laziness, suffered through a miserable live-in relationship and finally telephoned the A's employee-assistance department and said, "I want to get some help."

He found a therapist, learned to like himself, rededicated himself to year-round iron pumping and showed up at camp the next season with 20 pounds of new muscle.

Though McGwire did smash 42 home runs in that comeback year, it was also the first of five consecutive seasons in which he could not stay off the disabled list. He missed 40% of his team's games during that stretch; his enormously muscled body seemed to be too big for the rigors of playing baseball. A rib-cage strain, a torn left heel muscle, a sore lower back, a left heel stress fracture, a torn right heel muscle ... those seemed to many observers to be the natural consequences of a body made unnaturally large. Many, including opposing players, believe he uses steroids. He denies the charge. Vehemently.

Spending time with McGwire is a bit like a tour of his home. Things seem so tidy, so neatly arranged as to make one wonder: Isn't there something wrong with this picture? Well, yes, the bed is unmade. And with McGwire, in addition to the whispers of steroids, there is the question of leadership. As the star system crumbled around him in Oakland—Jose Canseco, Rickey Henderson and Dave Stewart were among those who departed—McGwire was unable to grow into the franchise's standard-bearer the way Tony Gwynn did with San Diego under similar conditions. When he left, McGwire irritated A's executives by crowing about how he had never seen anything like the support in St. Louis. Had he forgotten the glory years in Oakland, when he and Canseco milked their Bash Brothers image, turning themselves into beloved Bay Area icons? Wasn't it possible that if a dispirited, needy McGwire had been traded to Baltimore or Colorado, anyplace with a welcome mat, with "energy," he would have felt just as wanted and signed on there just as readily?

The last time McGwire's body gave out, two years ago, it nearly prompted him to leave the game. After his third foot injury McGwire felt he'd rather quit than go through another rehab.

Mark's favorite photo shows him relaxing with Matt in Mexico.

Friends and family talked him out of it. He missed 18 games that season and still hit 52 home runs, the first of his back-to-back 50-homer seasons— something accomplished only by Ruth and this 250-pound strongman who gets teary watching Jessica Tandy being driven around by a chauffeur.

His 2,200-square-foot home is as quiet as it is neat; he renovated the master bedroom suite on the second floor. The bathroom includes two sinks. One is raised four inches above standard height to better accommodate him; he doesn't have a girlfriend at present, so the other goes unused.

In the middle of the master bedroom, between his bed and a sitting area, is a great wooden desk from which McGwire E-mails his friends. Next to his computer is another framed picture, blown up to 8-by-10. "This is my favorite," he says.

Mark and Matthew are shoulder deep in a swimming pool in Mexico, where Mark took his son for his 10th birthday. They have their bare backs to the camera, their forearms resting on the pool's edge with their elbows out in exactly the same position. For all but the boy's first year of life, over too many miles and too many phone calls, Mark has been a divorced father. Now another man has stepped in to share the great and small responsibilities of fatherhood. But Mark can look at this picture and believe the serendipity of the image reaffirms an essential truth about him and his son—the same truth he sees in the fact that Matthew finishes his sentences, reads his thoughts, rips the low pitch and scuffles to catch up to the high hard one. Exactly like Dad. The photograph of Mark and Matthew was taken at midday, when the shadow we cast is a version of ourselves writ small.

21

From SI: 6/29/98

The Education of Sammy Sosa

Before the season began, several sluggers were seen as capable of making a run at Roger Maris's single-season home run record, but Sosa was not among them. By June, a month in which Sosa would hit a major league–record 20 homers, people had taken notice of the talented Chicago rightfielder.

By Tom Verducci

Sammy Sosa used to wear a millstone around his neck. It was a gold pendant approximately the size of a manhole cover, hung from a chain that seemed fashioned from a suspension-bridge cable. The bauble was inscribed with a drawing of two crossed bats and bore the numbers 30-30, inlaid with diamonds. The Chicago Cubs outfielder wore it when he drove to Wrigley Field in his sports car, the one with the SS 30-30 license plates. Then he would place the pendant in a safe before games.

Sosa had commissioned the Liberace-style accessory in 1993, after he became the first Cub to hit 30 home runs and steal 30 bases in a season, a milestone he reached thanks to 26 frantic stolen base attempts (20 of them successful) in the last two months. Never before, it seemed, had anyone been so ecstatic about finishing in fourth place.

What a piece of work! And the pendant, too—unintentional symbol of a vacuous career—was something to behold. Partly a creation of Wrigley Field's cozy dimensions, the notoriously undisciplined Sosa through his first nine seasons racked up nearly as many strikeouts as hits and approached his defensive responsibilities as if he thought "cutoff man" was a John Bobbitt reference. At week's end he had played 1,159 games without getting to the postseason—more than any active player except the Devil Rays' Dave Martinez (1,502) and the Indians' Travis Fryman (1,166).

Last season was vintage Sosa, beginning in spring training, when in response to a question about the possibility of his hitting 50 home runs, Sosa replied, "Why not 60?" His was most probably the worst year ever by anyone with 36 dingers and 119 RBIs. Behind that impressive-looking facade, Sosa hit poorly with runners in scoring position (.246), was virtually an automatic out on any two-strike count (.159), whiffed more times than anyone else in the National League (174), had a worse on-base percentage than Atlanta Braves pitcher Tom Glavine (.300 to .310), and again ran with such recklessness trying for 30-30 (he didn't get there, finishing with 22 steals in 34 attempts) that manager Jim Riggleman was once forced to scold him in the dugout in full view of the television cameras. Oh, yes—and the Cubs finished 68–94.

Sosa learned that his personal goals and those of the team could be reached with a single stroke.

24

Sosa's disciplined hitting and defense took time to develop, but the finished package was worth the wait.

"I think there comes a time in every player's career when he plays for the team and doesn't worry anymore about getting established or putting up numbers," says Chicago shortstop Jeff Blauser. Sosa's time is now. Buoyed by the best lineup that's ever surrounded him on the Cubs, Sosa has put together a monster first half as rich in substance as it is in style. At 29 and in his 10th big league season, Sosa has at last begun to take more pitches, hit the ball to the opposite field and realize that the only piece of jewelry that really matters is a championship ring. Only his numbers are gaudy now.

At week's end he was hitting .339—82 points better than his career average—and had cut down on his strikeouts, increased his walks and launched one of the most outrageous power streaks the game has known. From May 25 through June 21, Sosa slammed 21 home runs in 22 games. In four weeks he exceeded the career seasonal highs of every one of his teammates except leftfielder Henry Rodriguez.

What's more, in June's first 21 days Sosa hit more home runs (17) than any man ever hit in the entire month, blasting Babe Ruth (1930), Bob Johnson (1934), Roger Maris (1961) and Pedro Guerrero (1985) from the record book while closing in on the record of 18 for any month, held by the Detroit Tigers' Rudy York (August 1937).

He popped home runs like vitamins last week: three on Monday, one on Wednesday, two on Friday and two on Saturday. Of course, he hit all of them at Wrigley, where in the last three years he has hit twice as many as he has on the road (71 to 35). So hot was Sosa that teammate Mark Grace jumped on his lap in the clubhouse, rubbed against him and yelled, "Gimme some of that!" And that was *before* Sosa hit a 375-foot missile on Friday with a splintered bat and a 461-foot lunar probe Saturday—the June record-breaker—that crashed a viewing party atop an apartment building on Waveland Avenue. Just call him Babe Roof.

While Sosa wore out pitchers, the big payoff was that the Cubs were still hanging within four games of the first-place Houston Astros in the National League Central at week's end. For the first time in his life Sosa was hearing his faithful flock of rightfield fans chanting, "M-V-P! M-V-P!" More telling, when reporters asked him about possibly outgunning Ruth and Maris over the full season, Sosa rolled his eyes in embarrassment and said quietly, "Oh, god. I'll just let you people take care of that. I don't want you to put me in that kind of company."

Why not 60? This time Sosa said, "I'll let you know after the year is over."

Sosa has reached a comfort zone. That it took so long in coming should not be such a surprise. Not when you consider that he didn't play organized ball until he was 14. Not when you take into account that he grew up selling oranges for 10 cents and shining shoes for 25 cents on Dominican street corners to help his widowed mother make ends meet. Not when you learn that home for him, his mother, four brothers and two sisters was a two-room unit in what once served as a public hospital. Each

night when he put his head down on that wafer of a mattress on the floor, he didn't dream of playing baseball in a tailored uniform on manicured fields. He dreamed of his next meal.

The scout invited two kids to a field in San Pedro de Macoris for a tryout in 1985. Sosa was the one in the borrowed uniform and the spikes with the hole in them. He was 16 years old and carried only 150 pounds on his 5' 10" frame. The scout made a mental note that the boy looked malnourished.

The scout timed him at 7.5 seconds for 60 yards. Not great. The kid's swing was, by his own admission now, "crazy"—all long and loopy. But the scout liked the way the ball jumped off his bat, and he liked the way the kid did everything on the field aggressively. So the scout, Omar Minaya of the Texas Rangers, eventually made his way to the Sosa home ("No bigger than the average one-bedroom apartment or large studio," Minaya recalls) and came up with an offer of $3,500. Sosa took it. He gave almost all of it to his mother, Lucrecia, allowing himself one modest extravagance: He bought himself his first bicycle.

The following year he was at the airport leaving for some place called Port Charlotte, Fla., without knowing a bit of English. As he looked over his shoulder, the last thing he saw was Lucrecia crying.

Only three years after that—only five years after he took his older brother Luis's advice to play baseball—he was in the big leagues. By the time he was 23, Sosa was playing for his third team, the Cubs. The Rangers and the Chicago

25

White Sox each chose not to wait to see if he would acquire polish, trading him for veterans.

"When he first got here [in 1992], you could see he had great physical skills, but he was so raw," Grace says. "He didn't know how to play the game. He didn't understand the concept of hitting behind runners. He didn't understand the concept of hitting the cutoff man to keep a double play in order. So many little things he just didn't know."

This much he did know: If he was going to support his mother and family, it wasn't going to happen with the bat on his shoulder. "It's not easy for a Latin player to take 100 walks," Sosa says. "If I knew the stuff I know now seven years ago— taking pitches, being more relaxed—I would have put up even better numbers. But people have to understand where you're coming from.

"When I was with the White Sox, Ozzie Guillen said to me, 'Why do you think about money so much?' I said, 'I've got to take care of my family.' And he told me, 'Don't think about money. Just go out and play, and the money will be there.' It takes a while."

Midway through last season the Cubs provided Sosa, already a millionaire, with $42.5 million of added security by way of a four-year extension, a contract that astonished many observers. Sosa had never scored 100 runs, had never had 175 hits and had made fewer All-Star teams in the '90s (one) than Scott Cooper.

Sosa's record-breaking streak in June vaulted him into the thick of the home run race.

Atlanta Braves manager Bobby Cox refused to add him to the All-Star team in 1996 even though Sosa was leading the league in home runs at the break. Equally unimpressed fans had never voted him higher than ninth in the balloting. Even this year he is running only sixth among National League outfielders.

"We saw a five-tool player who was coming into what are the prime years for most guys, and who probably couldn't find the trainer's room because he's never [hurt]," says Chicago general manager Ed Lynch, explaining the thinking behind the extension. "The one important variable was Sammy's maturity as a player. We were banking that he would continue to improve."

Upon signing his new deal, Sosa did not buy a bicycle. He bought a 60-foot yacht that he christened *Sammy Jr.* By then he also owned, he says, "eight or 10 cars"—he can't remember exactly. Lucrecia is now living in the third house her son has bought for her, each one bigger than the last.

Cubs hitting coach Jeff Pentland gave Sosa a video to take home after last season, though he did so without great expectations. "I don't think he knew I existed last year," Pentland says.

The video included batting clips of three players: the Braves' Chipper Jones, Grace and Sosa. The tape showed that all three tapped their front foot on the ground as a trigger mechanism for their swing. But while Jones and Grace tapped their foot as the ball was halfway to the plate, Sosa would tap his when the ball was nearly on top of him, resulting in a wildly hurried swing. "We needed to come up with

some way for him to read and recognize pitches sooner," Pentland says, "and that way we'd be able to slow him down."

A few weeks later Pentland called Sosa in the Dominican Republic. "All I care about are two stats: 100 walks and 100 runs scored," Pentland told him.

"And one more," Sosa said. "I want to hit .300."

Not once in 16 straight plate appearances against Philadelphia last weekend did Sosa swing at the first pitch. (Last year he had 84 one-pitch at bats; almost halfway through this season he has 16.) Two strikes aren't deadly for him anymore, either. In those counts, he had improved to .232 with 13 home runs, four more than he hit in such situations all of last year. The tried-and-true strategy for retiring Sosa—getting ahead on the count and making him chase pitches farther and farther off the plate—no longer applies.

Every day before batting practice Sosa and Pentland meet in the batting tunnel under the rightfield bleachers at Wrigley. Pentland flips him baseballs to hit. He tosses them not on a line, as normally occurs with this drill, but in a high, slow arc. That way Sosa must wait, with his hands back, before finally unleashing his swing and belting the ball into a net where the right side of the field would be. The drill teaches patience. Sosa at last understands. The 30-30 pendant is a relic now, no longer found around his neck but in a display case at his home in the Dominican, like some artifact from another era.

27

From SI: 8/3/98

Home Run Fever

The second half of the season was underway when Gary Smith embarked on his homer-chasing pilgrimage. It was a three-slugger race then—Ken Griffey Jr. was still in the thick of it with 40 home runs—and Greg Vaughn was making his case for history, too.

By Gary Smith

You're out of it, pal. You're hungry, and the kitchen's closed. You don't live in St. Louis or Seattle or Chicago, where the story of this American summer of 1998 is cooking, nor in the other big cities where the dailies bring it piping hot to the breakfast table every dawn. You live a 5½-hour drive from the nearest big league ballpark, and your newspaper's serving it up like bulletins from the front in World War I—GRIFFEY HITS 39TH; SOSA'S 36TH LEADS CUBS; MCGWIRE MASHES 2 MORE—followed by a bare-bones sentence or two, and Christ, there's not even *SportsCenter* to fill your belly because your wife bears a deep grudge against TV and sneers whenever you creep down the stairs at 7 a.m. to turn it on.

But you're a sportswriter, and people assume you know. "What do ya think?" they ask. "Is Maris's record gonna fall? Which one's gonna do it? What kind of guy's McGwire? Who do you like?" You don't know who you like. Never met any of the three men in your life. It's scary, not being able to answer the watercooler question.

So you get this idea. It's too good to be true, but you ask your boss anyway. How about letting you chase the chase? Three cities, three nights, three men—go on a long-ball bender, a four-bag jag. Enter the bubble to feel what it's like to be one of them right now, belting homers and stalking legends. Then become one of the mob up in the seats, rising to snag history. Big Mac in San Diego on Monday, Junior in St. Petersburg on Tuesday, Slammin' Sammy in Chicago on Wednesday, back-to-back-to-back … pretty please?

Sure, says your boss. Why not?

Hot damn! You're going … going … *gone!*

It's only when you're up in the air at dawn, blinking on four hours' sleep and staring at the travel schedule you've scribbled out, that you start thinking, Man, this is lunacy, and what are the odds you'll actually see any of the big boys launch? Two flights, 2,500 miles and 14 hours later you're sitting in a football locker room next to the visitors' clubhouse at Qualcomm Stadium, waiting for the press conference that Mark McGwire holds on his first day in each city when he's on the road. You remember reading about the media horde that swallowed

Throughout the historic home run race, McGwire preferred to let his 33-ounce bat do the talking.

30

Sosa (left), McGwire (above, with his son, Matthew) and Griffey all found their own ways to relax in the midst of the home run race madness.

Roger Maris in 1961. Ten to 15 reporters would converge on him before and after each game. That was in September, when Maris had 55, 56, 57. Today is July 20. McGwire has 42. There are 30 of us.

McGwire walks in, dressed for battle. He sees the four cameras aimed at a chair and a table holding a half-dozen microphones. He shakes his head in disgust. "I'm not gonna sit down," he says. He leans against one of the lockers, his green eyes blinking like those of a cornered ox as the humans and their hardware close in.

Haltingly, the questions come. You have this feeling that if you ask the wrong question, he might chomp your head off, and you would absolutely deserve it, so you wait for someone else to ask it. "I don't know how anybody can get used to this," McGwire says. "I don't play the game for this.... The media sets this up like it's going to happen ... so how are they going to write it if it doesn't happen?"

Is he having any fun? "Between the lines, I have a lot of fun," he says.

The cameras and microphones reap the

20-second snip they need and begin peeling away, and as the crowd dwindles to a dozen men with notepads, McGwire's stiff, mammoth body loosens—the cornered ox is gone. He looks every questioner in the eye and answers earnestly. "I wish every player could feel what I've felt in visiting ballparks," he says. "The receptions I've received.... It's blown me away. It's absolutely remarkable."

You follow him into the Cardinals clubhouse, feeling bad because now you like him, and your eyes feel like cameras. There it is, blaring from the television that hangs from the ceiling and faces all the lockers—an ESPN segment on the home-run-swinging styles of McGwire, Ken Griffey Jr. and Sammy Sosa, the crack of McGwire's bat and the bark of his name coming over and over. You can't help feeling that here's a guy who wishes to hell he could do this without expectations, without the dread of letting people down.

You're startled, as you follow McGwire down the tunnel to the dugout, to hear the cries begin even before he emerges. "McGwire! McGwire!" He walks past the bleating fans, never looks up. Every head, every camera is on him. His face is a mask, eyes gripping a nothingness before him.

Two hours before game time, the leftfield stands are choked with people wearing mitts. The air crackles. Foul territory is thick with writers and photographers and special guests—a hundred, easy. There's George Will and his two sons. "It's not about the pennant races any-more," Will tells you. "It's about the home run race. You'd think I'd want Sosa, because I grew up a Cubs fan, but I'm rooting for McGwire.... But all three of them seem to be nice human beings. There's not a Sprewell in the house."

Three of them? Or is it four now? You look up, and there's San Diego Padres outfielder Greg Vaughn standing 10 feet away. His 34th home run, yesterday, has brought him within two of Sosa, to the lip of the volcano, and since you're here, hell, why not nudge him in too? He gives you a big, warm, no-way-in-hell grin and says, "I won't even think about it. I don't want to hear or see anybody blowin' smoke up my butt."

McGwire strides to the plate for BP. You park yourself right at the rope that keeps non-combatants back from the cage. Everyone's on his feet. A couple of grounders, *ohhhh*, a couple of fly balls, *ahhhh*, and then the thunder, *whoooooah!* Twenty-two compact swings in all, seven bullets into the sea of begging bare and leathered hands. Just before McGwire finishes, a boy runs out to the cage in a Cardinals uniform with McGwire's name and number on the back—Mark's son, Matthew, reporting for duty as batboy and Nation's Luckiest Child. Big Mac grins, slaps five and hugs the boy, then heads back to the clubhouse.

You go up into the stands, buy a soda and a hot dog, and grab an empty seat near the Cardinals' dugout. Big Mac approaches the plate in the top of the first to a standing O. He's not a Cardinal anymore. He's on everyone's team.

Camera flashes pop all around the concrete

31

bowl. McGwire lashes a white-blur single to left, Little Mac gallops out grinning to collect his daddy's shin guard, and you're thinking, Damn, wouldn't it be nice if your son could be beside you to see this, and how can you not root for this guy?

Bottom of the second. Vaughn launches number 35, which goes 433 feet to dead left. Look out, people tell you. Here comes Vaughny.

32

Sammy's 37th came close to these Sosa fans (above), but not as close as McGwire's BP shot to Colwell's cheek or his 43rd homer, which bounced off Conway's head and into Byers's hands (left).

Sitting on the third base side, watching that home run descend, you know where you need to go—on the double.

Second deck, that's too obvious. For Mac's third at bat, in the fifth, you guess first row, lower deck, pure rope, and man your battle station. Fool! There she goes—good god, they really are as long as you've read!—a 458-foot bomb into the second tier in left center, the second-deepest one since distances were first recorded in this ballpark. You jump to your feet with everyone else, jam your notepad under your arm and pound your hands together, hardly believing your good luck. You've got to find who snagged that baby, but when you get up there, it looks like a hospital tent at Shiloh. A silver-haired man is holding a wet folded paper towel to an ugly red welt high on his forehead. A seat away, a man with a Padres hat tugged over unruly blond hair is wincing and fingering a humdinger of his own on his left cheek. "We're victims of McGwire!" cries Bob Colwell, a 46-year-old machine operator from Ocean Beach, Calif.

"McGwire did this?" you ask. "To both of you?"

"To both of us!" shouts Colwell. "Can you believe it? I'm up here during batting practice explaining to [my girlfriend] about Roger and the Babe.... All of a sudden I see McGwire hit one that's coming straight for me, and it's like a scene from *The Natural,* it's surreal, and I'm wearing a glove, which I haven't worn in 20 years, thinking, I've got a chance! I reach up, but everybody bumps me, and it hits the top of my glove and then hits my cheek, and there I am bumming out, bleeding profusely, when I turn and ... there's my honey holding the ball! Thank God, thank God! Then what happens? Lightning strikes twice! The home run McGwire just hit? It comes right up here again! And this guy, who I didn't know before tonight"—the factory worker thumps attorney James Conway on the back—"this time he gets nailed! Do a story on us! Victims of McGwire!"

So who got number 43? you ask. They point to the row behind, where a thick 49-year-old high school football coach named Robert Byers Jr., from Moreno Valley, Calif., took it on the ricochet off Conway's noggin. "As I watched it coming, I just kept telling myself what I always tell my receivers," Byers says. "*Soft hands, soft hands.* I just turned down an offer of $700 for this ball."

Big Mac goes 4 for 4, with a walk. Cards win 13–1. What you want to do right now is go get a cold one with James and Robert and Bob, but there's no time for that. Junior's waiting back on the other side of the country, and the only way to get there in time for batting practice tomorrow in Florida is to take the red-eye, but it's 11 p.m., too late to catch the last flight to the East Coast out of San Diego, so you've got to drive two hours up I-5 to catch the 1:55 a.m. out of L.A. and change planes in Dallas.

Only nine of your kind surround Junior when he looks up, stick of red licorice poking out of his mouth, eyes cool, voice distant. You can touch the tension again, glimpse the cliff edge these three sluggers must walk.

"I don't like to talk about myself," he says. "Hard to believe, isn't it? I'm not going to talk about home runs. I just want to win.... It's hard for people to believe that Roger Maris's record isn't important to me, but it's not."

A journalist uses the word *chase.* Junior won't have it. "Only thing I wanna chase is my kids," he says. Nobody's going to pigeonhole him as a home run hitter when he's clearly the finest all-around player in the game.

"That's all people want to talk about," he says, "but 50 home runs will probably win you only 12 games a season. I think more about the little things, like playing defense, getting guys over—that might win you *40* games."

Whew, you almost blow it. Just before the fourth, you go grab a slice of pizza and rush back in when you realize Junior's fixing to hit. *Crack!* Number 40 goes screaming over the 407 sign in center, and the fans finally come off their cans to scream too. You drop your pizza box and almost pinch yourself—counting Vaughn you're 3 for 3!

Slammin' Sammy's next. The wild card in the deck. Holding at 36, he has jacked just one in the

33

last 11 days, but just might hit 20 in the next month, as he did in June. As your plane wings toward O'Hare and everyone around you is reading about the home run chase, you're wondering: Could you possibly go 4 for 4?

You enter the clubhouse 3½ hours before the Cubs–Montreal Expos game and find Sosa swaying to Latin music. "I'll take care of you," he tells you. "Just wait." Over an hour you wait, and when you finally get the nod, Sammy opens a magazine of local real-estate listings. Uh-oh....

Even for Sammy, who's never been a household name, the novelty's gone. He answers your questions lifelessly, eyes rarely lifting from photographs of houses with circular driveways and swimming pools. He says 18 minutes is enough. You resist recommending the brick colonial. What right do you have to be miffed? Jeez, isn't each one of these guys entitled to his own little way of hiding right in front of everyone's eyes?

The Wrigley fans are a whole different herd from the people you've met in San Diego and St. Petersburg. Everybody's got wit, everybody's got beer, everybody's got a desperate clear-eyed love for his team and an astonishing intimacy with it. Everybody's trying to decide whether he'll betray rightfield—*family*—and sneak over to left when Big Mac comes to town next month, and mulling how to stash an extra ball somewhere so that if Mac sends one into his palms, God willing, he'll have something to hurl back on the field when the mob chants, as it always does, "Throw it back! Throw it back!"

Here comes Sammy to take his position, bolting out of the dugout like a pitchforked bull, veering sharply at the warning track and acknowledging the bleacher bums' *Sam-my! Sam-my!* chant with a fist thump on his heart and a kiss to his fingers.

Amazing, how everything changes up here. With words out of the way, Sammy's pure heart comes shining through—he's the faithful mute using hand and body language to keep up a steady patter of appreciation for the legions behind him. Shouldn't he be the one you pull for to make history?

Sammy steps to the plate for his last poke in the home eighth, Cubs up 5–3. You look across the stadium to the poor guys sitting on their hands up in the press box and ask yourself why—if you ever cover a ball game again—you would do it from there. It's nuts here tonight, fans heaving balls at Expos players, fans racing on the field and dodging the diving tackles of security guards, fans raining beer cups on the field. Now there are runners on the corners, wind blowing to right, fans waving fish nets and thumping HIT IT HERE, SAMMY T-shirts, packed house on its feet, and you right there with them, thinking, No, these sluggers have already given you three homers and a combined 9 for 14— you can't ask for more.

Then more comes. Across the night sky it comes—impossibly, Sammy's 37th, straight at you. You're watching it, feeling the beer splash across your neck and the regulars closing around you like a fist. A fan throws up his hand in front of you and the ball smacks off the heel of his palm

Sosa's 37th brought jubilation to Wrigley Field as Crowley (in blue shirt) won the battle for the ball.

and bounces into the green mesh basket along the lip of the wall. Now it's a dogpile of flesh at your feet, everybody you've been drinking beer with diving and clawing and grunting. Marty Crowley wants it most. He goes headfirst into the basket, legs flying up before you, wrenches it from a crowd and comes up whooping.

You? You just stand there like a happy idiot as someone pounds you on the back and bellows,

"You did it! Three nights in a row! This is incredible! You sure you're not coming back tomorrow?"

No ... no, you're not. You're on an 8 a.m. flight home the next morning, looking like something the cat dragged in, wondering who it is you finally want to break the record. Your eyes begin to sag, and a smile comes to your lips as it dawns on you.

You've got the record. Nobody on the planet's ever going to see all four of the men assaulting history hit home runs on three straight nights—just let 'em try. Go to sleep, you tell yourself.... You've got it.... You've got it in the bag.

CGWIRE · 31 ATL 5 1/3 1 AND 1 OUT 2 ⑪ NEWS ⑪NINE 12 48
G .292 43 STL

History in Sight

History in Sight

By Merrell Noden

With the single-season home run record now obliterated by not one but two men, it is easy to forget those weeks in July and August when it seemed that Maris's record would escape once more, perhaps forever. Earlier, the mark had seemed sure to fall. By the All-Star break, McGwire had hit 37 homers, Griffey had 35, and upstart Sammy Sosa, who in the month of June alone had clobbered 20 homers—more than any man ever hit in a single month—had 33. Sure, one of them might tail off when the real pressure was applied, when they could no longer move without having a thicket of microphones thrust into their faces—but all three? Could they really all miss?

But in the weeks following the All-Star break that mighty trio faltered. In 35 games from July 11, when he hit number 38, through Aug. 18, McGwire hit just 10 home runs, and those neat little stat boxes, which seemed to have popped up magically in every sports section in the country, showed his projected total slipping almost daily, from a high of over 70 to 61. With an established history of second-half fades, it seemed quite possible McGwire would again fall short of Maris's mark.

Inspiration came in the form of Sammy Sosa, whose huge grin and goofy good nature were the lightning to McGwire's scowling thunder. The 29-year-old Dominican also had fallen off his early pace—how could he not, with a June like that?—but not as precipitously as McGwire. On Aug. 16 Sosa hit his 47th homer and caught up to McGwire for the first time all season. Two days later the Cardinals came to Wrigley, and what transpired there shifted the season into breathless overdrive. Sosa, who had been playing perfect possum, perhaps erred in hitting number 48 in the presence of his rival. If McGwire had ever really meant it when he said that the perfect ending to this season would be a record tie, he didn't act like it now. He waited just three innings to reclaim a share of the lead and two innings later took it outright with number 49. Sosa too caught fire, and when the pair began September with 55 homers apiece, Maris's record seemed sure to go.

For the next six weeks, their race became a national obsession. Hundreds of writers shadowed the pair, Ted Koppel sonorously analyzed them on *Nightline,* and ESPN cut to their every

Although McGwire (right) won the home run race, he and Sosa (above) will be forever linked in our memories of the 1998 season.

National League with 40 homers in August 1996 when he was hit by a pitch that broke his wrist and ended his season, Sosa had never hit more than 40 homers in a season. He had not been living for years under the awful burden of others' expectations, as McGwire had. He became the hero of underdogs everywhere, a shining champion to all Latinos, especially Dominicans. In the New York City neighborhood of Washington Heights, where Dominicans make up much of the population, delirious fans began painting Sosa's name and current home run total on car windshields and the sides of vans. The race took on added poignancy when in the final week of the season Hurricane Georges virtually leveled Sosa's hometown of San Pedro de Macoris.

Thanks to the seeming prescience of the schedule-makers, Sosa was in rightfield when McGwire hit Numbers 61 and 62. After respectfully allowing McGwire time to hug everybody in sight, from his own son, Matthew, to Maris's sons, Randy, Roger Jr., Richard and Kevin, Sosa ran in to add his own congratulations. It was a perfect tableau for an astonishing season: We all knew what home run madness looked like from the outside, but only these two men knew what it felt like from the inside.

turn at bat. With the realization that the home run balls would fetch staggering sums on the memorabilia market—the 62nd as much as a million dollars—it became a matter of life, death and sometimes the law to catch them. Those who did were whisked away by an army of security men and became instant celebrities—until the next home run. Lawsuits were filed disputing ownership, and the IRS even reared its ugly head, letting it be known that the tax codes applied to even national treasures like record home run balls. Facing a public outcry, the IRS backed off.

But the two principals rose above such pettiness. They were the perfect foils. What seemed to be an ordeal for McGwire looked like a lark for Sosa—surely because of the sweet unexpectedness of it all. Though he had been leading the

From SI: 8/31/98

48, 49, 50, 51, 52, 53...

With a five-day burst in late August, a joyous McGwire got over the 50-homer hump and made it clear that the question was no longer if *he would pass Roger Maris's record but* when.

By Tom Verducci

The most zealous of the believers—the 500 or so who had waited more than an hour in the 85° swelter for one last look—let out a roar when Mark McGwire walked out of Gate A of Three Rivers Stadium on Aug. 23 in Pittsburgh. They pressed against metal barricades with tidal-wave force. McGwire wore sandals, jeans, a batik shirt and the last thing you'd imagine from someone whose life has been a petri dish for six months: a smile. McGwire had two choices. To his right, the sanctuary of the St. Louis Cardinals' bus, with his teammates waiting in its cool interior behind the deeply tinted windows. Straight ahead, the zealots who have turned Cardinals games into revival meetings, a chance to worship the almighty long ball and have their faith in baseball restored. The gospel according to Mark.

What to do? Actually, McGwire had made the choice two weeks earlier. He headed straight into the maw of the crowd, grabbed a pen and began signing autographs. "There was a time when I wasn't in a good mood, probably said some things I shouldn't have said," says McGwire, who at one mass press conference chided reporters to "worry about your fami-

lies," not his home runs. "But I just decided about two weeks ago I was going to enjoy this. And I am."

That was never more evident than in late August. Beginning on Aug. 19 in Chicago, when for three innings he trailed Sosa for the first time this year, McGwire blasted six home runs in 19 at bats. That five-day burst gave him 53 home runs. McGwire needed nine home runs in St. Louis's last 32 games to break Maris's record.

"I have a legitimate shot," McGwire says. "It's a matter of getting pitches to hit. People talk about the pressure from the media. That's not it. It's the pitchers. That's what it comes down to."

McGwire's universal fan support may encourage pitchers not to pitch around him. Last month Cincinnati Reds fans booed Cincy pitcher Mike Remlinger when he left a game against the Cardinals in the eighth inning, even though he had a 6–2 lead. His crime? He gave McGwire nothing to hit, walking him twice and

Slump buster: After a drought—for him—of 20 at bats, McGwire went deep for a 48th time, at Wrigley.

hitting him with a pitch. Mets fans also booed their own pitchers last week whenever they fell behind McGwire 2 and 0, and 3 and 1. Fans are shaming pitchers into challenging McGwire.

"I'm not trying to walk him," says Pirates righthander Jason Schmidt, who nonetheless did so twice on Sunday. "It's exciting for me to go after him. Hey, I'm definitely rooting for him to break the record. If you're a baseball fan, you've got to be rooting for him, because of the person he is and the way he respects the game."

When he hit his 50th home run in New York on Aug. 20, McGwire punched the air with his fist (*opposite page*) and clapped his hands twice

as he rounded first base. "Never have I seen him show more emotion than that on the field," says St. Louis manager Tony La Russa, "and I've seen him hit a home run to win a World Series game. He doesn't let the door to himself swing open very much, but he did there."

On Aug. 20, McGwire became the first player to hit 50 home runs in three consecutive seasons. After adding his 51st home run in the second game of a doubleheader that night, he said in an emotional postgame news conference attended by about 100 media types, "I've got my second wind now." Then, after answering questions until none remained, he asked before leaving, "Is that cool with everybody?"

In Pittsburgh, McGwire slammed number 52 on Aug. 22 off righthander Francisco Cordova—a 477-foot bomb and one of only three home runs he has hit to the right of center-field this season. He launched number 53 on Aug. 23 off a 2-and-2 pitch from lefthander Ricardo Rincon and then sat out Monday's game, as planned. He has one more off day scheduled for either Cincinnati or Houston in September.

With every pitch McGwire sees, hundreds of flashbulbs pop in the stands. ESPN cuts into programming to show every pitch to McGwire. In Chicago a woman in the stands asked him while he was in the on-deck circle if he could verify that the McGwire jersey she bought for $200 on the

In the face of intense media scrutiny, McGwire and Sosa learned to sit back and enjoy the ride.

42

Internet was genuine. He told her it was a fake.

McGwire is under such scrutiny that the Associated Press broke a story last week—Flash: Baseball player uses a legal supplement banned by the NFL that's available at your local mall!—by "snooping in my locker," McGwire says, and spying a bottle of androstenedione, a natural substance that raises a man's testosterone level. McGwire says he takes the supplement three or four times a week, one hour before his weight lifting workouts "to get a better pump," as do "nine or 10 other guys on this team."

"There's always someone who wants to spoil the glory," says teammate Brian Jordan about the androstenedione controversy. "Just enjoy it."

In this so-called renaissance year for baseball, McGwire has single-handedly saved the game from a drop in attendance. The Cardinals' combined home and road attendance has increased 784,950 from last year, but overall major league attendance in games not involving St. Louis (or the two expansion teams) is down 118,783 from 1997. At $25 a head—based on the Total Fan Index survey average spent by a family of four at a ball game—the extra 6,000 fans McGwire brings in per game would mean an estimated $24.4 million in additional revenue for baseball by season's end.

His greatest contribution, however, could be heard on Aug. 23, when he stood in a tunnel next to the visitors' dugout at Three Rivers Stadium unhinging the protective guard from his left shin after hitting number 53. It was the sound of 42,134 true believers on their feet, cheering an opponent. "I felt uncomfortable," he says. "I'm a visiting player."

Rincon threw a pitch to the next batter, Ray Lankford, and still the cheering didn't stop. Finally, a few Cardinals pushed McGwire out of the dugout to acknowledge the crowd, as the Yankees had done with Maris after number 61 in 1961. McGwire recognized the faith he heard in those cheers. The summer has made a believer of his son, too. "It's fun to see him fall in love with the game," McGwire says. "The last year or two he really didn't care to play. Now, I see the smile on his face. That's the best part."

43

The Good Father

Rick Reilly's profile of McGwire appeared after Big Mac hit home run No. 55, just six away from Roger Maris's record. After years of self-doubt, McGwire finally seemed at ease with himself, with his feelings and with his role as a father.

By Rick Reilly

Huge men don't cry, but the McGwires do. This time it was John McGwire, 6'3", 225 pounds, the dad of slugger Mark, who was weeping. He was talking about the metal brace he has worn on his right leg for the past six years. He stopped and half started again and then stopped altogether. His strawberry face reddened, and now he had his glasses off, quietly weeping.

"I just collapsed," he finally said. "I was seven years old, walking across the floor of our house, and my legs just gave way." John's stepfather carried him upstairs and called the doctor, who made the dark diagnosis: poliomyelitis. This was in 1944, 10 years before the polio vaccine was successfully tested. John was taken to the contagious-patients ward of the local hospital, where even his own mother couldn't visit him. Every day, for six months, they would roll his bed over to the window, and he would wave to his mother on the sidewalk below. Then they'd roll him back. Now John was crying again.

Still, John McGwire wound up with a good life. He's 60, the father of five healthy brutes, one of whom is threatening to break baseball's coolest record as if it were a pair of chopsticks. Despite having one leg inches shorter than the other as a result of the disease, John became a prodigious bicyclist who still rides for an hour at a time 3 or 4 times a week and, for a while, an 8-handicap golfer. He even boxed in college. Yet he never told his sons in much detail the story of his polio, of collapsing in a heap, of waving to his mother. None of the five sons ever asked, and their father never told. Just recently Mark has learned to cry too, but he has never seen his father weep for that scared little boy. "We didn't talk about stuff like that in our house," says Mark. "We just didn't. Anything [emotional] I had like that, I always shoved inside."

And, from inside, it nearly ruined him.

If 62 happens, Mark McGwire will be hung from his heels and dipped in bronze. Paintings will be commissioned, many for the sides of skyscrapers. Already, at least five couples in St. Louis have named their newborns McGwire. If 62 comes along, towns will be next, perhaps followed by a few of the smaller states.

That's why you should know now that underneath the mask and cape is a person who often

Three generations of McGwires—John, Matt and Mark— shared in the excitement of Mark's historic season.

loses track of what day it is, has worse sinuses than Felix Unger and couldn't see a beach ball coming at him, much less a baseball, without the aid of science.

McGwire may be a 6'5", 250-pound duplex with pillars for forearms, but his lifestyle leans more toward branch librarian. He loves to spend nights at home watching The Learning Channel and sports a floppy fishing hat, which he knows he looks kind of dumb in but wears anyway. He doesn't wear near enough jewelry to drown (one necklace), and he's so hopelessly square that he's got only one measly car.

Besides, he's a complete doofus about money. Here's a guy whose face is all over the place, but he doesn't even have a shoe deal. "Too distracting," McGwire says. (This is the equivalent of the sultan of Brunei doing his own ironing.) Or any other major national endorsement deal. "Too distracting," he says.

He has turned down Letterman, Leno, *60 Minutes*, book deals, movie deals. You name it, he hasn't done it. "Too dist—" We know!

McGwire is claustrophobic, too. That explains why he hates being surrounded by the media. It's not so much the questions, it's the surrounded by. His press conference at the start of each road series attracts as many as 125 media types. As they close in, he looks like a man about to be interrogated by Turkish officials. If the crowd pins him against a wall, he fidgets. He rocks back and forth. He makes nervous faces, clicks his tongue continuously, scratches his nose, rubs his back against the wall, perhaps hoping to trigger a secret

Mark has become friends with his ex-wife's husband, Tom (with Kathy, Matt and 2½-year-old Shelby).

panel. But as the TV guys run out of questions and leave and the radio guys get their sound bites and go, he gradually calms down until, at the end, when there are only two or three writers around, he's merely miserable.

That also explains why in June he lashed out at the "circus" that batting practice had become. He said he felt as if he were in a "cage," which, of course, he literally was. For a claustrophobe, all those reporters, cameras, club officials, teammates, teammates' kids and opponents gathered around to watch him seed clouds must have made the batting cage feel like a cardboard box with holes cut in it for viewing.

And his feet! Lord, they're the two ugliest this

side of Sasquatch. "Duck feet," he calls them. They are unusually narrow at the arches and then, suddenly, splay out into bouquets of rosy rumpled toes. He's also considering suing his arches for nonsupport, since they led to heel and foot injuries in the mid-1990s.

Yet people tend to think he stood up in the crib at three months and started smashing the planets on his mobile into the hallway with his rattle. Wrong. He's been through acres of hell. He came down with mononucleosis during his sophomore year in high school, which led him to quit baseball for a while and take up golf. He nearly quit again in 1985, when he got off to a dreadful start during his first full season, with Class A Modesto. "I can remember lying in bed in the middle of the night," says his ex-wife, Kathy Williamson, "and Mark saying, 'I can't hit the baseball anymore. I'm done. I've lost it. I've got to quit.'"

He's been through a divorce, self-doubt, self-loathing, a waiting room full of injuries, and slumps you wouldn't wish on a French waiter. "I was all closed in," he says. "I didn't like myself. I wasn't a very secure person. I could never face the truth. I always ran from it. It's like, sometimes I look back at myself in those days and think, Who the f--- *was* I?"

Then one day, tears streaming down his face, he found out.

What Mark McGwire is doing right now is one of the great achievements in the history of sports, not just because he, like Sammy Sosa of the Cubs, is closing in on Roger Maris's record of 61 home runs in a season, but also because he's breaking it with the kind of power that causes 50,000 people to display their cavities in unison.

Even if he happens to hit just 61, his 61 will have traveled a medium-length interstate farther than Maris's. Used to be, a 400-foot shot would cause men to write songs and hang plaques. McGwire's home runs this season have *averaged* 425 feet. A guy goes through his career, he's lucky to have hit the longest ball in *one* stadium. McGwire has hit what are believed to be the longest bombs at Busch in St. Louis (545 feet), the Kingdome in Seattle (538) and Qualcomm in San Diego (458). His batting practice dingers have done more harm to major league cities than urban decay. He inflicted $2,000 worth of damage on a scoreboard at Bank One Ballpark in Phoenix. He thumped one off a stairway railing on Waveland Avenue, outside Wrigley Field in Chicago. He has cleared the roof at Tiger Stadium in Detroit. At Coors Field in Denver he hit one that ricocheted among the fully loaded Range Rovers in the players' parking lot.

This isn't like hitting a golf ball 350 yards. This is a baseball coming in at 90 mph with sick spin on it from the whipsaw arm of a strong man pushing off an anchored rubber on a hill 60' 6" away under artificial light with 50,000 people screaming and another 100 million waiting to read what happened in the morning paper. "Do you know how hard guys are trying to get me out?" he says, exasperated. "I see the best, every AB." Ted Williams said hitting a baseball is the hardest thing to do in sports. Try having to hit one to Peoria.

47

And to think McGwire has built this Taj Mahal out of popsicle sticks and chewing gum. No other great home run hitter has seen so few decent pitches. With 141 bases on balls, including 27 intentional passes, McGwire was not only on pace to break Ruth's season record of 170 walks, but he also had an outside chance to break Willie McCovey's record of 45 intentional walks. (Maris, by the way, had zero in 1961.) This season the San Francisco Giants intentionally walked him with nobody on. Then there are the de facto intentional walks. "I guarantee you, 30 percent of the walks he draws aren't listed as intentional, but they might as well be," says Dave McKay, who's the Cardinals' first base coach as well as BP pitcher.

Says Cardinals manager Tony La Russa, "If they'd just pitch to Mark, he could hit 80." The problem is McGwire actually looks for the walk. Of his 55 home runs through last weekend, only one was on a 3-and-1 count, none on 3 and 0. "We tell him, be more selfish," says La Russa, "but he won't."

This isn't new. As a boy, McGwire would stash his trophies in the back of his closet, not on top of his dresser. They embarrassed him. On the form for the media guide at USC, he left the space next to athletic honors blank. Most sports stars have double lockers to handle the overflow of mail, gifts, freebies and reporters. He's got a single. The man doesn't even own his rookie card. No interest.

One day when Mark was a boy, he gave his shoes to a friend in need. He gave away his baseball gloves, his shirts, a sweater once. These days, he's still giving, only a little bigger. He donates a million dollars a year to a fund for sexually abused children. Now strangers walk up to him and tell him stomach-turning stories of sexual abuse. Says McGwire, "Sometimes I'm just speechless."

All this free and open discussion of secrets, troubles and emotions is fairly new to him. You didn't do it in the McGwire family when he was growing up. Besides, who had time to talk when there was only so much time to eat? All five boys ended up at least 6'3" and 220. They were all killer athletes—Dan was a quarterback at San Diego State and later played for the Seahawks and the Dolphins, Mike played high school soccer and golf, Bob was a standout for the Citrus (Glendora, Calif.) Community College golf team. Then there was Jay, the baby. Jay was an unhittable pitcher, a deadly shooter in basketball, a welt-raising linebacker. "He was better than me," says Mark, a star pitcher and golfer in high school. "I always told him that."

Then, when Jay was 15, a BB fired from an air rifle bounced off a tree and hit him in the middle of his right iris, blinding him in that eye. He tried to keep playing, but it was hopeless. "The accident kind of put Jay into a spin," says Williamson. Jay tried competitive bodybuilding. He got seriously cut, good enough to finish sixth in the Mr. California contest, but it wasn't a wonderful life. He was taking now-banned body-building drugs and working out eight hours a day. "It worried me,"

McGwire's focus in BP (above) is intense, but Matt (below) can always provoke a smile.

Mark says. "I wanted him to get on with life."

At the same time, Mark's own life started dissolving. He'd married Williamson, the USC batgirl, just after he was the 10th player picked in the June 1984 draft, and she got pregnant two years later. But in '87, after he hit the big leagues with the Oakland Athletics, batting .289 and roping a rookie record 49 home runs, the marriage unraveled. "I think there were too many things calling Mark's name," she says. "Women, fame, glamour."

They separated, tried to get back together and then split for good just as the 1988 World Series began, A's versus Dodgers. McGwire went 1 for 17. Oakland lost in five games. Kathy and Mark's son, Matt, was one.

McGwire's batting average and home runs

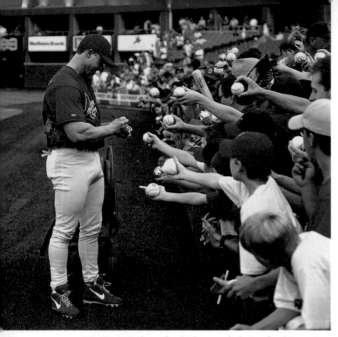

McGwire's love for kids—and theirs for him—is evident in every ballpark he visits.

sank over the next three seasons, and he finished 1991 hitting a skinny .201, with only 22 homers and 1,000 self-doubts.

In those days, when you tried to interview McGwire, what you mostly got was a great view of his back. He never opened up. "I was kind of a wreck," he says. "I was having all kinds of relationship problems. I didn't know what love was all about. I had four brothers and no sisters. We never talked about it. You're never taught: These are how feelings are. It's like you're walking into a dark room and just feeling blindly around."

It's not easy for big guys to ask for help, but when McGwire walked into his house after the

1991 season, he threw his bags down, went to a phone and called a therapist, whom he saw for the next four years. "It took failure for me to understand myself," he says.

Jay moved in with Mark, and they helped each other. Jay left bodybuilding, became a devout Christian and is now a successful personal trainer. "I'm so proud of him," says Mark. "He's the happiest guy in the world."

Living with Jay, Mark learned how to lift weights the right way and stay flexible. Mark would work out six days a week in the off-season, four during the season. He lifts after home games now and is routinely the last to leave the clubhouse. Before games and workouts, he stretches for an hour. He does eye exercises. Whenever he goes to a restaurant, he knows the protein count of every meal, of which he usually orders two.

He decided to stop being a guess hitter and start being a smart hitter. During the two years, 1993 and '94, when he was able to play only 74 games because of injuries to his left heel, he began to sit behind the plate with the scouts and study pitchers. He changed his swing to finish with a one-hand extension for more power. He learned to close his eyes and hit. Not during the game—the night before, visualizing where the pitch might come and at what speed. "Just take what they give you," Doug Radar, one of his hitting coaches with the A's, told him. That became McGwire's motto. He becomes so focused on the game that most days he has no idea what day or date it is. "I'm useless during the season," he says.

Not really. "It's hard to even compare him

now with any other time," says La Russa, who also managed McGwire in Oakland. "He's so much better now. He's better conditioned. His swing is quicker. His stroke is much more repeatable. Now, he thinks all the time."

But, most of all, he discovered a missing father. Himself. "Everything I do in life and in baseball now is for my son," Mark says, and that's obvious from the small Olan Mills gallery that has broken out all over his locker and in his home. Photographs of Matt, now 10, are everywhere. As far as Mark is concerned, every day is Take Your Son to Work Day. The Cardinals let Matt be a batboy. Mark had it written into his contract that Matt has a guaranteed seat on any team charter. Do they talk? They never shut up. "We talk all the time," Mark says. "We talk about everything. If there's one thing I've learned, you have to talk. We talk so much that sometimes we don't even have to use words. We just look at each other and know what the other is thinking."

Matt lives with his mom full time, and Mark wants it that way. Besides, Mark's house in Orange County is only five minutes away. He has become friends with Kathy's husband, Tom Williamson, a manager in the collision repair field. You go over to the Williamsons' house in the off-season, you're likely to find McGwire hanging, all of them grilling burgers or playing golf.

This man's a red-whiskered Ruth—a huge thing, pitcher turned hitter, nuts about kids, colossal eater and making his greatest mark in the 50th year after Ruth's death, as if to memorialize him. "Babe Ruth?" McGwire says. "That's crazy.

People bringing me up with Babe Ruth. It still blows me away."

Still, it's one nasty record, and it gave Maris blotches on his skin and globs of hair in his comb, and it gnaws at McGwire sometimes. "I'll say to myself, What am I getting so stressed about?" says McGwire. "The Man Upstairs knows what's going to happen. I totally believe that, and that takes the pressure off." *Just take what they give you.*

"I had bad karma going for a while in my life, but I think I've learned," he says. He wants to help people. Recently he dated a woman who worked at a home for sexually abused children, which led to his $1 million-a-year donation, which was announced last fall—with his new Cardinals contract—at a press conference, during which he choked up, stopped talking and cried openly on camera.

"You know, they'll run that sometimes, and it still amazes me," he says. "It took crying for me to realize, This is the real me. That day, when I cried, is when I realized I can open up. I can care. I can communicate. I sometimes wonder why so many people have become drawn to me, and I think that's why. They saw me as a real person after that. It took crying to make me realize who I am now. I'm the Mark McGwire I'm supposed to be."

And who's that?

"What do you mean?" he says.

Who are you?

"Well, I'm—I'm an opinionated, understanding, communicative, sensitive … father."

Touch 'em all.

51

From SI: 9/14/98

Record Smasher

McGwire hit his record 62nd home run on Sept. 8, 1998, in St. Louis, with Tom Verducci looking on. But Big Mac was by no means finished; he would add eight more by season's end.

By Tom Verducci

He was 20 years old, a member of the touring 1984 U.S. Olympic team and two summers away from his first major league game when he opened the door for the first time to the redbrick building at 25 Main Street in Cooperstown, N.Y. But then something odd happened as Mark David McGwire stepped across the threshold of the Baseball Hall of Fame. He stopped cold. He found himself saying aloud to himself, "I'm not ready for this history." And then he abruptly turned around and left—and hasn't been back.

Fourteen years later, with an adoring nation held spellbound, his time arrived. McGwire made a permanent place for himself not only in Cooperstown but also in American folklore. On Sept. 8, 1998, McGwire broke the most mythologized, most revered and most American of sporting records. He hit his 62nd home run of a season that has rekindled the country's interest in baseball.

Sixty-one, a number that needs no introduction, has lost its magic. Its owner, the tragically poignant Roger Maris, has lost the single-season record after 37 years of ownership. McGwire's blow, a bases-empty shot off Steve Trachsel of the Chicago Cubs, occurred two days before what would have been Maris's 64th birthday.

Earlier in the day the stock market soared 380½ points, the first day of trading after a Labor Day weekend in which McGwire hit number 60—measured at 381 feet—and number 61. Coincidence? Who knew anymore, not after McGwire himself had marveled at his accomplishments in this season of serendipity.

The home run is America—appealing to its roots of rugged individualism and its fascination with grand scale. Americans gape at McGwire's blasts the same way they do at Mount Rushmore, Hoover Dam and the Empire State Building. "We have," Cubs manager Jim Riggleman said before the historic game, "a fascination with power."

How deliciously ironic, then, that the biggest home run of McGwire's record season turned out to be the shortest of his 62, a 341-foot piece of sweet simplicity. McGwire stepped into the batter's box with two outs and no one on base in the fourth inning at 8:18 p.m. CDT, having stuck to his unwavering on-deck routine. He doesn't take practice swings. He's a man of

On the second at bat in his 137th game, McGwire turned Trachsel's fastball into a historic shot.

McGwire was so excited after parking No. 62 that he missed first base (above); but once he had touched them all, the celebration began (right).

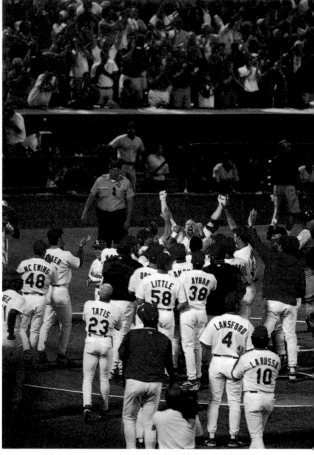

reserved ferocity. He swings the bat to inflict damage upon a ball.

In the first inning Trachsel had induced McGwire to ground out to shortstop on a 3-and-0 pitch—a hitter's count on which McGwire had not hit a home run all year. This time he decided to start McGwire with a first-pitch sinking fastball, exactly the sort of pitch McGwire devours. The ball arrived at 88 mph, accompanied by the usual strobe show of fans' camera flashes.

McGwire lashed at the pitch, sending it so low toward the leftfield corner that he sprinted out of the box, thinking it would stay in the park. The ball cleared the wall by about five feet and only three feet in from the foul pole, the 12 ball—in a set of 48 specially numbered balls

prepared by Major League Baseball for all of his at bats after his 59th homer—into the corner pocket.

The ball caromed off an advertising sign and dropped into a field-level concourse that rings the stadium under the seats. A groundskeeper, Tim Forneris, fetched it and ran through the concourse to the Cardinals' clubhouse.

"I got the ball! I got the ball!" he yelled to equipment manager Buddy Bates. Bates ran it into his office, closed the door behind him, put it into a wall safe and called baseball security officials. They quickly arrived with a black bag containing a black-light lamp. When they turned it on and placed the ball under it, it glowed with the invisible ink devised specifically for the occasion.

Just after the ball went over the wall, McGwire reached first base and leaped into the arms of coach Dave McKay with such excitement that he bounded over first base. Laughing, he retraced his steps and touched the bag. The entire Cardinals team greeted him at home plate. Also there was his 10-year-old son, Matthew, in his pint-sized uniform holding his father's bat. Mark picked up his son and held him so high aloft, the helmet fell from Mark's head. Soon McGwire ran to the first row of seats next to the St. Louis dugout and hugged Maris's children. The Cubs' Sammy Sosa, his home-run-race rival, who had become comedy-team partner, soul mate and adopted little brother to McGwire during this chase, ran from rightfield to embrace him.

Meanwhile, someone threw a ball on the field marked with a number 3, the Rosie Ruiz of baseballs. Somehow that ball made it to McGwire. On one side of the ball was a message: GOTCHA. McGwire, though, saw only the words "Official League" and knew right away it was a phony. "Take it back," he told a security officer. McGwire had huddled with two representatives of the Hall of Fame two hours before the game in the Cardinals' clubhouse, the same

clubhouse where Maris had dressed during his last two seasons in the big leagues. He vowed his cooperation with the Hall in donating his paraphernalia from the record home run. Then Jeff Idleson, the Hall's director of communications, showed McGwire the 34½-inch, 32-ounce bat Maris had used to club his 61st home run in 1961. McGwire clutched the bat, rubbed the barrel over his heart and said, "Roger, you're with me." Now McGwire stands alone.

After the game, McGwire presented the Hall of Fame the ball, the bat used to hit homers 56 through 62, his full uniform, spikes and hat, and the jersey his son was wearing. The Cardinals presented McGwire with a red Corvette—a '62, of course—during a ceremony at second base. McGwire invited the Maris family to join him in the ceremony. Randy Maris, who was born in the summer of '61, wiped a tear from his eye as he stood with his three brothers and two sisters. "It was sad," Randy explained, "but Mark's such a great guy, what can you say? The guy deserved it. We never thought we'd see this day come. That's why I was sad."

The day came earlier than even McGwire expected—in St. Louis's 145th game. "All the pressure that's been on him," teammate Tom Lampkin said, "and I haven't seen how it has affected him at all. Amazing."

America is a Baseball Nation again, and McGwire is its head of state. Every time he marches to the plate at Busch Stadium in St. Louis, every fan in attendance rises to his feet out of

55

As his teammates waited to congratulate him, McGwire hoisted his son, Matthew, who was happily clutching the record-breaking bat.

with his 715th homer, were that his skin was black and that he had batted 2,900 more times than Ruth. It escaped Maris, too, when he hit 61 homers in '61, because he had played eight more games than Ruth did while hitting 60 in '27, leading commissioner Ford Frick to devalue Maris's accomplishment with an asterisk. Maris suffered, too, because he was not an anointed descendent in the Ruth-DiMaggio-Mantle Yankees dynasty. It didn't help that neither before nor after '61 did he hit even 40 home runs in a season. "I think it's great for Mark," Randy Maris said last weekend about the country's support for McGwire, "but you sort of wish Dad had had the same thing."

Neither asterisks nor animosity weighed on McGwire. He's the rightful heir to one of sport's great crowns, an ascent that began with his birth on Oct. 1, 1963—two years to the day after Maris hit number 61 off Tracy Stallard. "No one ever told me that growing up," McGwire says. "I just never knew until recently."

He arrived in the big leagues in August 1986, eight months after Maris was buried under a tombstone engraved with 61 and '61, and almost immediately he was seen as a threat to the home run record. In '87, his first full season, he smashed 33 homers before the All-Star break. "The questions about 61 go all the way back to then," he says.

Even before this season began McGwire was expected to endanger Maris's mark: He had improved his totals in the three previous years from 39 to 52 to 58 and, like Maris, would have

respect and awe. Virtually all Americans cheer him with a loving acceptance that sadly escaped the two men before him who drove Babe Ruth from the record book. It escaped Hank Aaron, whose crimes against the ignorant in 1974, when he broke Ruth's career home run mark

expansion-team pitchers to feast on. He hit a grand slam on Opening Day, hit another home run the next game and the game after that and the game after that, and soon he became baseball's answer to the Dow Jones, only without weekends off.

McGwire defied the conventional wisdom that as in scaling a mountain, the closer a hitter drew to the home run summit, the more difficult the climb would become. Beginning on Aug. 19, with a pair of homers against the Cubs at Wrigley Field, McGwire mounted a furious three-week charge at Maris. He cranked out 15 home runs in 66 at bats. Through Sept. 8, either McGwire or Sosa had homered on exactly half of the 158 days on which games were scheduled—including 15 of 21 starting with that tête-a-tête at Wrigley. "What's amazing is that they're making it look easy," said Cardinals second baseman Delino DeShields last Saturday. "It's not easy, man. That's a gift."

Said McGwire after hitting number 61 on Sept. 7, "I have been thinking about the record since I reached the 50 plateau. But you think about it, and then you let it go because you can't waste many brain cells on hours of thinking about it."

His humility and respect for the game have made McGwire a national treasure, which is why Major League Baseball assigned two detectives to protect him around the clock when St. Louis is on the road. They were guarding him even as he lunched at Chuck's Steakhouse in Fort Lauderdale on Sept. 1. They watched him (without incident) eat steak and chicken, pound two home runs that night and then order up the same fare the next day: steak and chicken followed by a double dip of dingers. That binge put McGwire at 59 heading into a five-game homestand. On the eve of that series, during his only off day in a month, McGwire spent eight hours at Busch Stadium filming a public service announcement designed to help stop sexual abuse of children.

Number 60 came on Sept. 5, a sweltering afternoon. There was one out and one runner on in the first inning when umpire Larry Poncino gave Cincinnati Reds lefthander Dennis Reyes one of the four dozen baseballs reserved for McGwire's at bats. Baseball security officials, working with the U.S. Treasury Department, had marked the balls so that McGwire's 60th home run and those thereafter could later be authenticated. They covered them with an invisible ink that glows when placed under an infrared light. They also put a small black numeral, from 1 through 48, on each ball beside the S in RAWLINGS.

Poncino gave Reyes ball number 2, the same one Cincinnati pitcher Scott Sullivan had used to strike out McGwire the previous night, but Reyes asked for another. "It was too white," he said after the game. "It didn't have enough mud rubbed on it for me. I have small hands, and if the ball is too white it feels slippery."

So Poncino gave him another. On the third pitch with ball number 3, McGwire tied Ruth, the great number 3, and became the third man ever to hit 60 home runs in a season. The homer

bounced among frenzied fans in section 282 in left until 22-year-old Deni Allen grabbed it off the ground. Allen gave it back to McGwire in exchange for two autographed bats and a cap.

McGwire already had bettered a number of Ruth's accomplishments this year (fastest to 400 career homers, most consecutive 50-home run seasons and most home runs over two and three consecutive seasons), but the 60th homer, hit in the 142nd game of the season, made it clear that McGwire is the closest thing to Ruth ever seen. "I really truly believe he's up there watching," McGwire said of the Babe.

Home run number 61 would provide more chills. After a homerless Sunday game, McGwire dined with his family and friends, including his father, John, who would turn 61 the next day. "Wouldn't it be something?" Mark said, as they talked about the possibility of tying the record on his father's birthday.

"If I could do 61," John said, "you could do 61."

The next morning Mark put off a phone call to John to wish him a happy birthday. "As I was driving to the ballpark I said, This is meant to be, to give him this birthday present," Mark would later say.

One important person was not yet in place, however. Mark's son, Matthew, arrived at Busch Stadium from California on Sept. 7, 14 minutes before the first pitch. He raced to the clubhouse, donned his batboy uniform and hustled to the Cardinals' dugout, getting there after the Cubs had batted. Mark was reaching into the bat rack to get his bat just as Matt got there. The father smiled at the son and said, "I love you." Then he bent and kissed him.

At 1:21 p.m. McGwire stepped into the batter's box and one minute later propelled a pitch from 38-year-old righthander Mike Morgan into the history books. The baseball

McGwire ripped a Morgan fastball to tie the record (left); the next night he celebrated the record-breaker with Maris's sons, Randy (above, left) and Roger Jr.

flew close to the leftfield foul pole, but McGwire threw his arms up in celebration even before the ball banged off the club-level facade. The man knows his homers, having hit more than 400 of them. The 37-year pursuit of Maris was over.

Some Cubs congratulated McGwire as he ran around the bases. Sosa clapped his glove in rightfield. Mark touched home plate and pointed to John in the stands behind the backstop. "Happy birthday, Dad!" he yelled.

"Last year I gave him a card," Mark said with a laugh after the game. "Now you tell me—is all that fate, or what? The man upstairs has a plan for me, I guess."

About two weeks earlier a fan left a voice-mail message for Reds manager Jack McKeon, whose team had walked McGwire 11 times in six games before this series started. "Please pitch to McGwire," the fan pleaded. "This is what we need. This is what the country needs to help with the healing process and all the trouble that's going on in Washington. This will help cure the ills of the country."

"So," said McKeon, "I did my part for the healing process. We pitched to him. I'd feel a lot better if someone said pitching to him helps the stock market."

For the moment, political and financial woes—not to mention the malaise that has beset baseball in recent seasons—were all forgotten as three generations of McGwires shared their joy in front of us: John, leaning on his cane, a man who could not play baseball because of a childhood bout with polio; Mark, hugging his chubby-cheeked son in those arms as massive as bridge cables; and Matthew, grinning wildly, one of many who fell in love with baseball for the first time in this special summer.

Right then you'd have to have had a heart made of tin not to believe in the power of baseball, and you didn't need to hold one of those glowing balls in your hands to feel it. This one belonged to John, a gift from a son to his father. A happy 61st indeed.

Sixty-two would belong to the rest of us, a welcome touchstone in a cynical age. That's the good news according to Mark.

59

Sam the Ham

Ebulliently stalking the Babe and Big Mac, bashing baseballs and merrily mangling his adopted lingo, the Cubs' fan-friendly Sammy Sosa was having the time of his life—on and off the field.

By Steve Rushin

At Carolina Panthers home games, fans are forbidden to remove their shirts and vendors call out "Cold beverage!" instead of "Beer!" At Chicago Cubs home games, shirt removal is compulsory, the better to show off a Ruthian beer gut. So we ask you, America: Which sport is truly your national pastime?

Baseball is back, and that has much to do with Chicago and the delightful space ranger who plays rightfield for the Cubs. Between the two estimable men competing for the single-season home run record, the 29-year-old Sosa is somehow the more human, no? While Mark McGwire ingests creatine and androstenedione, Sosa is popping body-enhancing Barneys and Freds: A box of Flintstones chewables sat on a shelf of his locker in Pittsburgh.

Here's a man who makes $10 million a year but doesn't play golf. "I tried one time to golf, and I hit everything foul ball," he explains. "I hit it over trees, over houses." Who cannot relate?

Of course, in baseball Sosa is hitting everything fair ball, everything long ball, having homered in 15 consecutive series through Monday, 58 times in all. Barring injury, he will

This tenth season of Sosa's career has been the most productive—and the most fun.

get to 62 but probably not before Mac Daddy gets there, which doesn't seem fair. "Let me ask you this," Cubs first baseman Mark Grace said after Sosa hit his 57th. "What are we supposed to do if Sammy hits his 62nd when McGwire already has, like, 64? Do we mob

60

him, even though 62 is no longer the record?"

Odds are the Cubs will mob him, in the way that Sosa is mobbed on his rare walkabouts in airport terminals and hotel lobbies. "Some of the stuff he hears, it would floor you," said Sosa's agent, Tom Reich, intriguingly, after dining out with his client in Pittsburgh. "Some of the people who approach him got balls. And I don't mean baseballs."

Of course, they got baseballs, too. The fan at Wrigley Field who caught Sosa's 56th home run personally returned it to Sammy after the game. Sosa signed the ball and gave it back. "It was a woman," he explained gallantly, "from the right-field bleachers." Sosa treats Wrigley's rightfield bleacherites with a reverence he otherwise reserves for his adopted homeland, the United States.

While McGwire can appear constipated in press conferences, Sosa has used them to hone his lounge act. "If somebody wants to have an interview with me," he says with a shrug, "it's a free country." On rare occasions Sosa will decline to answer a question by saying, "That's personal," though when he was asked last week to name his first love, he replied, without hesitation, "Cartoons."

It would be easy to see Sosa as a cartoon were it not for the three-dimensional depth of his emotions. Having shined shoes and sold oranges and played baseball with a tree branch and a rolled-up sock as a child in the Dominican town of San Pedro de Macoris, Sosa is sincere when he says of the U.S., "I love this country. Whatever happens to me now, I think it's a

gift." Believe him when he tells you, "Every day is a holiday for me."

Which raises the question, Why isn't McGwire this glib in interviews? Sosa blushes, bounces his eyebrows and ventures, "I'm a little bit more Rico Suave than him." At that, 25 cynical scribes—and Sosa himself—laugh for a solid minute.

His teammates do, too. Sosa spews out fun like a bus does fumes. "I feel he's a nice little treat that's been given to me at this stage of my career," says 40-year-old Cubs third baseman Gary Gaetti, who spent the first five months of this season with McGwire and the Cardinals. "I have no problem talking graciously about either of these men, because they're both great people."

Indeed, on Sunday evening in Pittsburgh there already was an elegiac quality to Sosa's season, a sense of things-will-never-be-like-this-again. As the Cubs prepared to get out of town, only 30 reporters were gathered at Sosa's locker. (Some 700 would await him in St. Louis.) As that number dwindled to a dozen or so—a reeking scrum of B.O. and dandruff, held together by giveaway golf shirts—Sosa shook hands with each of them. He said "Gracias" to the guy from Univision and, in short, showed gratitude to everyone on the media B-list, those assigned to follow Sidebar Sammy instead of Cover Boy McGwire.

"My life," Sosa reflected at one point, "is kind of like a miracle." For a moment everyone in his orbit—armadillo-skinned agents, 40-year-old third basemen, sneering sportswriters—felt the same way. It made you want to take off your hat and hand it to Sammy Sosa.

61

From SI: 9/21/98

The Race Is On

Although Sosa passed Ruth and Maris shortly after McGwire had already been there, done that, the season—and the race for the record—wasn't over yet. With a dozen games left, Gary Smith's story heralded Sosa's achievement, almost lost beneath the McGwire media machine.

By Gary Smith

Where was the commissioner? Where were the 600 media members? Where were Roger Maris's sons? Send the word! Tell 'em quick! Sammy did it too!

Where were the 350-bucks-a-bleacher-seat scalpers? Where were the Blue Angels screaming over the stadium's rim? Where was America looking last weekend when Sammy Sosa of the Dominican Republic belted four baseballs over the ramparts and through the palace door to halt the coronation of Mark McGwire?

Where were the zillion camera flashes last Friday night when Sosa hammered number 59 out of Wrigley Field and onto Sheffield Avenue? Where were the major-network cameras last Saturday when Sammy crushed number 60 onto Waveland Avenue? Where were the balls with infrared markers in the fifth inning on Sunday when he walloped number 61 onto Kenmore Avenue? Where, oh, where was the '62 Corvette when four innings later he poleaxed number 62, onto Waveland once more, in the wildest game of all, a 10-inning 11–10 Cubs triumph?

For 34 years Babe Ruth's record of 60 home runs shimmered in the distance. For 37 years Maris's mark of 61 went untouched. McGwire's record 62 stood alone for 116 hours. Then Sammy tied it and cried.

The race is on. To the split-screen finish Baseball's greatest individual race ever, seemingly spent after Big Mac went on a seven-homer in seven games jag that climaxed with his historic shot on Sept. 8, has its second wind, 10 miles per hour to dead left.

People piled into the streets in the Dominican Republic to celebrate Sosa's 62nd, tears streamed down grown men's cheeks at Wrigley, and the thunder of 40,846 fans took six minutes and three curtain calls to subside ... as baseball officials, sports editors and TV producers everywhere gulped hard.

No need to squirm. Don't bother alibiing. Don't try to explain away the disparity between the national response to Mac's 62nd and Sammy's. Don't open America's chest and search for rotting racial reasons why the Caucasian is creaming the Hispanic in magazine covers and slo-mo replays—well, all right, go ahead, but not now. Sammy wouldn't want it.

63

With a hot bat and little fanfare, Sosa served notice that the home run record was still up for grabs.

Sammy loves the cool of Big Mac's shade. Don't you dare blow his cover.

He has drafted behind McGwire for nearly three months, tying him for the fifth time on Sunday but nudging ahead of him only once—for three innings of a game on Aug. 19—making sure at all times to lean over Big Mac's shoulder and blow kisses and hosannas in his ear. Sosa's other camouflage, of course, is the Cubs' quest for the National League wild-card berth. Who but Sammy could tie Ruth one day, becoming the first non-American-born or nonwhite player ever to belt 60 in a season, then tie Maris and Mac the following day and watch both games end with bench-emptying, game-winning, bear-hugging home run celebrations at home plate … for someone else? Orlando Merced's three-run jolt won Saturday's heart attack, then Mark Grace's solo shot in the 10th closed Sunday's, and it was almost as an afterthought, after the Cubs lifted Grace to their shoulders, that Cubs catchers Tyler Houston and Scott Servais hoisted the man who had just thunder-struck baseball. Then Sosa ducked into the Brewers' clubhouse to thank manager Phil Garner for pitching to him—as well he should, after feasting on Milwaukee for *10* home runs this season—and stepped before the media, eyes glistening, to coo at Mac again.

"I'm so emotional right now," said Sosa. "Mark, you know I love you. It's been unbelievable. I wish you could be here with me today. I know you are watching me, and I know you have the same feeling for me as I have for you in my heart." He did the signature Sammy Sosa heart thump and added, "That's for you, Mark."

He had second-fiddled for Mac in St. Louis on Sept. 7 and 8, stroking just a pair of singles as America toasted McGwire. He applauded Mac. He hugged Mac. Then he ambushed Mac, breaking a 23-at-bat, five-game homerless silence with four weekend bombs that gave him 148 RBIs for the year, kept the Cubs one game ahead of the Mets in the wild-card race and likely salted away the National League MVP award.

Truth was, Big Mac wasn't watching Sosa either. When Sammy's 61st screamed 480 feet to left, McGwire was sitting in the trainer's room at Houston's Astrodome, where his Cardinals teammates were watching the Cowboys-Broncos game on TV. As Sammy's 62nd, off Brewers reliever Eric Plunk, pulled the Cubs to within 10–9 in the ninth and Sosa thumped his heart, kissed his fingers and mouthed the words "I love you, Mama" to a TV camera, McGwire was working up a pregame lather in an indoor batting cage.

"I think it's awesome," Mac said when reporters delivered the news. "I've said a thousand times that I'm not competing against him. I can only take care of myself. Imagine if we're tied at the end. What a beautiful way to end the season." He then took the field, hit two ground balls to short—making him a homerless 1 for 14 since the champagne bottles popped—and left the game when his back muscles, like America's heart, went into minor spasms.

Moments after the Sunday game at Wrigley, Major League Baseball tried desperately to scoop up the ball it had dropped. Commissioner Bud

Some gave Sosa the edge down the stretch because the Cubs were in the thick of a wild-card race.

Selig and Maris's son Randy placed phone calls as swiftly as cheeks blush and electrical impulses travel. Selig, who lives in Milwaukee, 90 miles north of Chicago, pleaded that he and baseball's brass couldn't follow two men all over the country, that the first man who walks on the moon is the one who gets the parade and that Sammy, too, will receive the new Commissioner's Historic Achievement Award, which was presented to Big Mac five days earlier. But how, given one hasty glance at the numbers, could so many have been gazing *there* instead of *here*? Since May 24, when McGwire had 24 home runs to Sosa's nine, Sammy has hit 53 to Big Mac's 38.

John Witt wasn't caught napping. On a small TV in a friend's van outside Wrigley, the 29-year-old Witt watched number 61 leave the yard, then turned and saw it bouncing toward him. Give it back? Unlikely. He was just divorced, he said, nearly broke and had already received a five-figure offer. Number 62 set off a free-for-all in which a man named Gary Mullins claimed he had his hand bitten while the ball was wrenched away from him. Another man, Brendan Cunningham, emerged from the melee with a ball and fled down an alley before police swept him away for his own protection. Because baseball officials hadn't treated the ball with the infrared markers that had been used to identify McGwire's historic homers, the gnashing might well have been for naught.

The possibilities, as we hurtle to the end of the home run chase, are delightful. After Monday night, when neither man homered, McGwire had 12 games remaining and Sosa had 11—unless the Cubs finish deadlocked with the Mets or Giants in the wild-card scramble and play a 12th game to untangle the knot, in which case any home runs he hits will count in the regular-season statistics.

Who has the edge, psychologically: McGwire, whose team is out of the running, or Sosa? "I've heard people say Mark has an edge because his team's not in a pennant race," said Cardinals manager Tony La Russa on Sunday. "I don't agree. Don't you think there's more energy before a game in their clubhouse than in ours?"

One thing, and only one thing, is sure: We won't be fooled again. Thump our hearts and hope to die.

Where Do I Go from Here?

In an exclusive account of his historic feat, McGwire reflected on his quest for the most revered record in sports.

By Mark McGwire with Tom Verducci

66

It took me only three days to find out that people look at me differently now that I've broken Roger Maris's record. I was shaking hands with some kids and adults sitting near the field before our game against Houston at the Astrodome last Friday night, and I kept hearing some of them shout, "He touched me! He touched me!" That blew me away. Two months ago nobody said that. That tells me people have changed their perspective on me, and it's something I'm going to have to deal with.

I hope people don't think, Well, he's a different person; look what he's done. I'd rather they think, That's just Mark McGwire; he did something historical, but, hey, he's just like us.

The way people across America have treated me this year, it's almost as if we broke the record together. People told me, "I can relate to you." Well, they did because I'm just a normal guy, because I show emotion and because I care about other people, especially children. So just because I broke the record, please don't lose sight of the fact that I am still all those things.

This is what I wish: that when I go home to Southern California after the season, my life will be the same as what it was before the record. I want to walk into the same public gym where I've always worked out, say hello to some friends, get my workout in and go home. Is that possible? I hope it is.

I know the opportunities for endorsements and appearances are pouring in. The day after I broke the record my adviser and good friend, Jim Milner, told me, "There's no way I can handle all of this." So we had to hire a public-relations firm just to field all the calls. But I told Jim, "Don't even mention a thing to me until a week or two after the season." Then I'm going to be very, very careful about what I consider.

I'm not going to allow any opportunities to take my vacation time away. I want to relax. I want to play some golf. It's the sport I played first, since I was five years old—my handicap's 10 now, because I haven't been playing much, but it's been as low as four. My golf swing actually comes more naturally to me than my baseball swing.

I really want to enjoy being with my son, Matthew. My birthday is Oct. 1; I'll be 35. His is three days later; he turns 11. For the past few

McGwire paused to give thanks but realized, "Hey, I've still got two weeks left in this season."

years we've taken a vacation together to celebrate our birthdays. Last year we went to Mexico. This year we're going to a special place, which I'll keep quiet. I'm very sensitive about Matthew's being in the public eye. I understand people are going to look at me differently and place more demands on me. But, please, leave my son alone. Let him be a child.

Last Thursday was Matthew's first day of school. When Kathy, my ex-wife, drove him there, she found a crew from a tabloid TV show waiting for him with cameras rolling. That's not right. It's a shame, and I hope nothing like that happens again.

It's only been in these past few days after breaking the record that I've realized the impact I've had on people's lives. I've received telegrams, letters and phone calls from Pete Rose, Johnny Bench, Joe Morgan, Cal Ripken, Jack McDowell, Brett Favre, Greg Norman, many of my former Oakland teammates and so many others. Ken Griffey Jr. hired an airplane to pull a banner saying congratulations when we were in Cincinnati. It's incredible.

See, I knew I had support, but I was so focused on what I was doing that I didn't realize it affected people the way it did. I was given a talent to play this game. I have the utmost respect for everybody who plays it, and to get that back in return, and to hear what people inside and outside baseball are saying, that means so much to me. It's unbelievable. So, thank you to everybody from the bottom of my heart.

The media's full-court press continued after No. 62, as each successive homer set a new record.

But as soon as I reflect on that support, I quickly tell myself, Hey, I've still got two weeks left in this season. I want to finish the season strong. The first day in Cincinnati after I broke the record, I didn't even know where I was. The second day, I was sort of coming back to earth. Then in Houston, over the weekend, the Astros just pitched me tough. In the first two games I saw one good pitch to hit—and fouled it back. But I have no doubt that in these last two weeks I can get back to where I was and get locked in again.

A lot of people ask me if I think anyone will make a run at the record next year. I don't know. I can't answer that until the end of the season, when I know what the final number is. I do know that there are five or six guys who will always hit between 40 and 50 home runs, and any one of those guys is capable of getting to the next level. I've always said the best way to look at it is you have to average about 10 home runs per month. That's consistency. But being that consistent is the hardest part.

I hit a little rut in late July and early August. That's not unusual for me. In past years when I've played a lot, I've gotten tired about that time and then found a second wind and had strong Septembers. What happened this year is that I got caught up in playing every day, because if I did take a day off on the road, the fans would get upset. I should have been thinking, O.K., what will help me stay healthy for the whole season?

I think I missed two or three days off that I normally would have taken, so some fatigue began to set in. I was struggling, and everybody was asking, "What's wrong with Mark? He hasn't hit a home run in 29 at bats or something." I got a little edgy. I said, "What are they worried about? There are things in the world to worry about other than Mark McGwire trying to hit a homer."

I probably shouldn't have said some of those things at the time. But then again, I was just being who I am. Other players read some of that stuff, and in early August guys on other teams came up to me and said, "Hey, just relax. Enjoy this. Enjoy the ride. What you're doing is great for the game."

I sat back and thought about it and said, "These guys are right." Sometimes somebody has to knock you in the head.

Some people think being around Sammy Sosa in Chicago for a series on Aug. 18 and 19 turned me around. But I made the decision to go ahead and have fun with this before that Cubs series. I will say this about Sammy: You can't help but see

the way he reacts to the attention. I think Sammy enjoys it so much because nobody really talked about him before. All of a sudden he hits 20 jacks in June, and the next thing you know he's right here. He's one funny individual. How can you not play off him? It just so happened that we got together right around the time I was starting to enjoy it. I changed my mind, and then Sammy was there. He made me think even more, Hey, this is fun. This is a game we love to play.

Baseball allows the media into the clubhouse up to 45 minutes before a game. I learned I couldn't even sit in front of my locker without someone tapping me on the shoulder and asking, "Got a minute?" So I made it a point to get some quiet time for myself. I'd find a back room where the media were not allowed, and I'd sit by myself and collect my thoughts and just get myself together. It worked. No music. No teammates. I'd just be relaxing. One of my real good friends, Ali Dickson, taught me how to do it— sort of meditation exercises. She showed me that this was a way to get myself grounded again. I call it tunnel vision.

Ali's on the board of directors for my charitable foundation, and it so happened that I had 59 home runs when she came to St. Louis on Sept. 3 to help with a public-service announcement I filmed for the prevention of sexual abuse of children. The next day the Cardinals began a five-day home stand. That's when my family started calling, asking for plane reservations and hotel rooms in St. Louis. I was saying, "You know, guys, I don't know when I'm going to hit a home run. They've been pitching me pretty good, even though I've hit a few home runs the last few days. I'm facing the Reds, and they've pretty much had my number all year, and then there's the big series against the Cubs. I don't know."

They still wanted to come out anyway, so I had all this added pressure of trying to do something in front of family and friends. If you were able to take an X-ray of my insides over the past two weeks, I'd hate to have seen it. My insides were churning. Yes, I was feeling nervous and feeling the pressure and trying to understand that the whole nation was watching.

But the funny thing is, I was only nervous up until the first pitch. When the game started, I was in the flow of it. All of a sudden everything was O.K. It came down to what I've always done: Get a pitch to hit, and try to put a good swing on it. That's what happened.

On the morning of Sept. 8—having had a good night's sleep after hitting my 61st home run on my father's 61st birthday—my stomach was turning the moment I woke up. I didn't like that feeling. It was out of character for me to feel that way right at the start of my day. I chased away that feeling, though, by relying on my routine. I'm very superstitious.

All I was thinking about while driving to the ballpark that day was, This is my last day here on this home stand. What a way to give something back to the fans of St. Louis for the way they've treated me since coming over here—to get number 62 at home.

The night turned out to be just perfect. Well,

almost perfect. If I could change anything about that night, it would be hitting a home run that didn't shock me so much when it went out. I had been so used to hitting balls well out of the park that after I hit the pitch from the Cubs' Steve Trachsel, I thought, That's off the wall. I've got to get going.

The next thing I knew, the ball disappeared, and I was in shock, I was numb. *I did it!* I had all these things running through my mind, and I was just floating in outer space. I can't even remember everything I did. I do remember I saw Matthew and I saw my teammates, and all of a sudden I was just standing there acknowledging the crowd when I glanced over and saw the Maris family. I just took off to their box and hugged them and told them that their father was in my heart. I hadn't planned it. It just happened. I knew what they were going through and the feelings they were feeling.

I was so happy that my mother, father and son all were there. And it meant so much to me to have Kathy and her husband, Tom, there. She's seen me go through so many things—all the way back to college, the minor leagues and my first couple of years in the big leagues. She's watched me grow as a person and as a baseball player. She told me some things in private that night that really touched me. I got very choked up.

Before the game in which I hit number 62, I met with two representatives from the Hall of Fame and told them I would turn over to them the bat and ball from the record home run. After the game I said to myself, You know what? What good is it going to do for me to have the jersey or the batting gloves or even my shoes? So right after the game I told them, "Listen, guys, you've got everything off my back." I gave them everything. That's where the history of the game is. It doesn't belong in my house. It belongs in the Hall of Fame. At least I know it's safe there.

I've kept nothing for myself so far. I've always loved to give things to people and see smiles on their faces. I gave the jersey I wore when I hit number 61 to my father. I gave the bat I used to hit numbers 50 through 55 to Jim Milner, who's been a second father to me. They both were speechless. You know what? That makes me feel good because those people have been there for me since Day One.

So where do I go from here? My next big career goal is to hit 500 home runs. I have 449 now. Somebody said I have a shot at 755, Hank Aaron's alltime career record. I think that's too far away for me. I will say this: How high my career total climbs comes down to my health. If I stay healthy like I have the past few years and I put up the numbers that I'm capable of, who knows how many more home runs I'll hit?

Anyway, I'm too focused on finishing this season strong to worry about the years ahead. I'm not surprised that Sammy tied me at 62 on Sunday. Not for one minute did I ever think this was over. No way. I've said before there are two weeks left in the season, and that's a long time. Anything can happen. It's like a horse race, with the horses jockeying back and forth. What it comes down to is, who is hotter at the end.

The experience of chasing the record was often as exhilarating.

I have a couple of goals that I want to reach this year: I'd love to bat .300, though I was only at .290 after Sunday and have to get on my horse to get there. The other goal is closest to my heart. It's something private between Matthew and myself. On the day before I left for spring training this year, I asked him, "Matt, how many homers do you want me to hit this season?" He told me a number—a number that's within reach.

What is it? I won't tell you. For now it's still a secret between father and son. But you'll probably be able to tell if I get there. After that one, I'll have tears in my eyes.

From SI: 9/21/98

The Mother of All Pearls

With McGwire's home run balls becoming more valuable than Beanie Babies, it was remarkable to find many fans willing to return the "pearls" to Big Mac in exchange for little more than a couple of bats and jerseys. Gary Smith wove baseball folklore from the fans' quiet decency.

... and there it lay, the great pearl, perfect as the moon. It captured the light and refined it and gave it back in silver incandescence.... It was the greatest pearl in the world.

—JOHN STEINBECK, *The Pearl*

By Gary Smith

Even now, in my wrinkled years, I cannot help myself. Each time I hear the crack of the bat I am there again, screaming and throwing up my arms with the mob, in that long-ago summer when the giant cast his pearls into the sky. Everyone, of course, knows the story of the giant, but the tale of the people who caught those pearls is one I don't tell so often anymore. No one believes it, and I am far too old to suffer cackles and clucks.

I remember carrying my glove in one hand and my fishing net in the other, joining the 50,000 who surged toward the coliseum on the riverbank in September of the year nineteen hundred ninety-eight. In stadiums all across the land, the giant had already driven 59 of those five-ounce spheres over the faraway fences. He was marching toward history, toward the magical sums of 60 and 61 that giants from decades long before had smote, and each sphere he socked into the rabble's hands

became more precious. Wealthy men wished to possess one to attract attention to their corporations or their causes, to display it beneath thick, impenetrable glass or to hide it in a vault and say, *It is mine.* Mc? I still don't know my motive or precisely what I would have done had luck tapped me. I just thought it would be wonderful to reach up and pluck a pearl from the sky.

Two offers, each of a million dollars, had been made for the Largest Pearl, number 62, and surely those just before it, as well as those just after, would be worth tens or hundreds of thousands. No more than 4,500 seats existed in the region of the stadium where the pearls would most likely land—far better odds than any lottery offered—so you can guess what happened. Shrewd men gobbled them up weeks in advance and sold them to us romantics and pearl diggers for $150 one day ... $250 the next ... $350 the third! So strong was the lust for these pearls that people feared for our safety. Pleas for calm were issued, along with the suggestion that a net be placed above the fence to

The unselfishness of fans who retrieved McGwire's home run balls may someday be recounted as fable.

catch the pearls and save us from ourselves. Guards and policemen were posted at every aisle and ordered to race to the spheres' landing sites and protect the people who captured them.

What made this all the more intriguing, and more wondrous too, was that another warrior, wearing another team's colors, was stalking the giant, just a few clouts behind. Depending upon what this stalker did, the value of the spheres could change hourly.

Further complicating matters, the giant had requested that his pearls be returned to him rather than sold, so that they might be placed in a museum in a distant rural town where others might view them. He wanted them back for *free*—he would pay nothing other than a few bats or jerseys on which he would ink his name. Money would corrupt the quest, he felt, and oh, what a fevered discussion this loosed on the streets, in the taverns, around the breakfast tables. Many people concurred with the giant because they loved this gentle man who gave vast sums of money to unfortunate children, who spoke of spirituality and karma and of how purity was repaid with purity. But it was all so confusing, because … well, I needn't remind you that the quest was occurring in a land whose fiercest opportunists and entrepreneurs were its icons and leaders. Don't ask me how, but it happened: A game had turned into a national referendum on the price of a man's soul.

By god, cried one soul, anyone who found a pearl worth a million dollars owed it to his children and their college educations to cash it in—

We climbed into the seats to shout ourselves hoarse, each a child again …

those were true family values. Yes, chimed in others, hadn't the ballplayers and owners already trampled on the purity long ago, turning themselves and their teams into commodities that jumped from city to city, wherever more cash was offered, and hadn't they even called off the games completely when their demands weren't met just four summers before? But the pearl belongs to the giant, others kept insisting. Well, some allowed, they might sell it, but they'd be sure to give a fitting portion of the money to charity. "This town is just stupid," a man sitting in front of me finally snorted. "Everybody is too nice. It's like winning a lottery—how can you give it back?" And none of their words meant anything, for no one truly knew what he'd do until the pearl lay in his hands.

How can I bring you to feel what we felt,

pulling cameras and painted bull's-eyes and gloves—old cracked ones and shiny new ones—out from under our seats each time the giant approached the white-lined box to make his attempt? We climbed onto the seats to shout ourselves hoarse, pounding fists into our leather, each of us turning into a child again. Nerves jangled in my belly: Could I handle it if he whacked one to me? Behind me sat a woman from South Korea who had seen herself catching the Largest Pearl in a dream. Beside me, on three straight days, sat men who had flown from Japan to reach for it. We shook hands, we talked and laughed … but one flick of the giant's wrists could turn us into enemies, all.

The sun was murderous on the days when the titan launched numbers 60 and 61, as if God had placed a magnifying glass over the stadium to inspect the heart of every man who inhabited it. It's not important for you to know that 50 seconds before number 60 hissed over the fence, I was standing at the very spot in the aisle where it landed. All you need to know is that while an usher was sweeping me away, another man, craftier than I, was evading guards and lurking just inside a portal, then diving on the pearl as eight or nine others piled on him, pounding and clawing. All you really need to know is what he did with it.

He was Deni Allen, a handsome fellow just out of college. He pushed the sphere inside the right pocket of his shorts as police whisked him away. He still played Wiffle ball with his pals and had vowed to them that he would return the pearl to the giant if he caught it; those were the morals his mother and his Southern Baptist church had poured into him.

But suddenly, with the pearl his, he entered an altered state: People looked at him and treated him in a way they never had. Officials whispered in his ear, photographers snapped his picture, reporters peppered him with questions, producers begged him to appear on their shows, strangers begged to touch his hand. Even with police protection, he looked over his shoulder—no telling who might come at him for the pearl. He closed his eyes and set his teeth and shook his head as even his grandfather asked him to consider all the justifications for keeping the sphere or selling it. When the game ended, he did what those who had caught pearls 56, 57, 58 and 59 had done. He handed it back to the giant.

He knew the next morning, when he lay in bed half asleep, shuddering as he dreamed that he still possessed the sphere and that hands and voices were coming at him from every angle, that he had done the right thing. I'll never forget his words: "It would've burned a hole in my heart if I would've hung on to it."

Number 61 ricocheted off the window of a restaurant in the faraway seats, split open the finger of a man who reached for it, bounced just a lunge or two away from where number 60 had landed … and came to rest under the seat of a 28-year-old man from St. Louis named Mike Davidson. This fellow tucked the pearl under his shirt as police shepherded him to safer quarters, but he never once paused to puzzle over his dilemma. He recalled that distant relatives had once won a lottery, that their lives had been ruined by all the money grubbers who had sprung from the woodwork and that they were never heard from again. Besides, he loathed having people's eyes upon him; his wife gritted her teeth every time she lifted a camera and he ducked. His voice was flatter than a dial tone, and he kept the red cap of the titan's team tugged low over his hairline. "I'm a lifelong Cardinals fan," he said. "This means more to him and to baseball than a million dollars does to me. Why be greedy?" He couldn't wait to give the pearl to the colossus and be left alone so he could get some sleep before he arose at 4 a.m. to slice cold cuts and dice vegetables in his job preparing food. "Had the spotlight, done with the spotlight," he muttered to all those clawing and cawing behind him.

I still don't know. Maybe goodness gathers more goodness, like a snowball rolling downhill: Six men in a row had now returned their pearls. Maybe goodness isn't goodness at all, but fear—fear of change, fear of the moral pressure that had mounted as each pearl was returned, fear of stepping before the blinding lights and relentless questions and saying, "I don't care what the others did, I'm keeping it, I'm selling it, it's mine." Maybe the fans, who had screamed for years over what had been done to the bond between them and the players, were putting their pearls where their mouths were. Perhaps it could've happened only in that city, with its heartland values, and for that giant ... I just can't say.

A few hours before the Largest Pearl was launched, I remember, I took a walk. Now the ante had been raised to a million dollars, but I couldn't stop thinking of a fable by John Steinbeck that I had read, about a man who found the world's largest pearl and dared to dream of how it might lift his family out of poverty ... only to be consumed by the jealousy of neighbors and strangers, pursued and attacked until finally his child was killed over the pearl, and the man flung it back in the ocean. I stopped at a park where office workers sat smoking at a picnic table. They all said they'd give the pearl back, but half said it after a deep sigh. I moved to another park a few blocks away, where four men sat on a bench swigging beer and vodka, one with a quarter in his left ear. They were unanimous. "You crazy?" yelped one. "Give that mother back? In their hearts, everyone wants to sell it—they're just afraid to say it now. Nobody wants to go down in history as the one man who sold it, but what they don't realize is he'll go down in history as the one man who had sense."

It frightened me that evening, the frenzy that ensued when one of the players tossed a sphere up into the seats three rows behind me. Men and women dived for it, while under their weight screamed a seven-year-old boy. Perhaps the Good Lord himself grew unnerved by the human experiment He had hatched. Perhaps He touched the giant's bat and kept number 62 from reaching us. It streaked just over the fence, into a storage area below the seats, where a member of the crew that groomed the stadium grass and

"It would've burned a hole in my heart if I would've hung on to it," Allen said.

dirt pounced upon it just before his brother did.

The young man's right hand went numb. His body trembled. Management of the giant's team had told employees that anyone who caught a pearl could do with it as he wished. But the man who held the Largest Pearl was a 22-year-old named Tim Forneris who grew up fielding grounders and imitating Cardinals in his back-yard and called the giant "Mr. McGwire." He had been an altar boy, a magna cum laude grad-uate of a Jesuit university, a volunteer at a homeless shelter. Even as he reeled across the field during the celebration, the pearl throbbing in his pocket, he bent to pick up the litter thrown by the euphoric mob.

His brother, Tino, also a groundskeeper, had

asked him to stop and think—of a *million dollars,* of the lifetime of struggle and toil he might detour. "Dirty money," Tim said later. "It would brand you to sell it. It's sad to hoard things. Life is all about experience, which I have here tonight."

I remember wondering if what the people in the faraway seats had done would touch the players and the owners the next time a new city and an extra million dollars in income beckoned. I remember people snickering at me. I remember a scribe in one of the grandest gazettes calling the man who returned the Largest Pearl a dupe—no, it was "a pigeon." But what man, I ask, can truly judge what another man must do in order to sleep soundly at night and look into the mirror in the morning?

The streak by then had reached seven, and nearly three weeks remained for the giant to swat more pearls. The final one was expected to be worth another million. What happened next, you ask? Maybe the people just kept returning the spheres to him, maybe not—after the Largest Pearl, even I stopped counting. All I recall is that a few days later, when the other warrior hit his 61st and 62nd, they went clean out of the park and *neither* was returned imme-diately. The man who gathered number 61 on the avenue behind the stadium held on to it to consider his options, while number 62 set off a ferocious street scrum in which one man lost the ball to another after his hand was bitten—and thank god for these people, thank god. For I am thick-skinned and fool enough to tell a fable ... but certainly not a fairy tale.

Sammy: You're the Man

When Michael Bamberger visited Sammy Sosa in mid-September the slugger was in an 0 for 17 slump and his Cubs were battling the Mets for the NL wild-card berth. In the ensuing weeks, a third team, the San Francisco Giants, would join the wild-card chase, and Sosa would break out of his HR slump, but not fast enough to catch McGwire.

By Michael Bamberger

In the wee hours of Friday, Sept. 18, 1998—on the day his youngest child turned one—the hero returned home. Sammy Sosa had just flown in from San Diego, where the Chicago Cubs had won three of four games from the Padres. He rode the elevator to the 55th floor of his building, on Navy Pier in downtown Chicago, a contented man: He was rich; the Cubs had a one-game lead over the New York Mets in the National League wild-card race; he had 63 home runs, the same as the other guy; and his new glasses, with heavy black Harry Caray–style frames, had been receiving excellent reviews.

Sosa reached his apartment. It was nearly two in the morning, and he was expecting a sleeping household. He opened the door, and there they were, very much awake: his mother, his wife, an aunt, his four brothers and two stepbrothers, his two sisters, along with other family members and friends. Most of them were fresh arrivals, visitors from the Dominican Republic. In the bedrooms Sosa kissed his four sleeping children. In the kitchen, he saw prime meats, ripe fruit, fresh vegetables. He hugged his guests.

In time, Sosa made it to the north end of his sprawling apartment. The three air-conditioning units in his bedroom were on full blast. He turned on the oscillating fan to circulate the frigid air. He's a man of simple tastes. Sleeping in a cold room is one of his joys.

When he woke up late Friday morning, Sosa knew what was coming, and so did the rest of his adopted city: the final home stand of the Cubs' absurdly entertaining season. At Wrigley Field on three consecutive afternoons—Friday, Saturday and Sunday—the Cubs would be playing another relic of the Midwest, the Cincinnati Reds. At stake was a berth in the playoffs for the Cubs and the most glamorous record in American sport for Sosa: most home runs, season. Sosa ate a heaping plate of beans, rice and avocado and went to work.

Fans streaming off the El at the Addison Street–Wrigley Field stop saw a sign posted by the Chicago Transit Authority: THERE MAY BE SLIGHT DELAYS WHEN SAMMY SOSA'S AT BAT. In the Cubs' dugout, another newly minted baseball philanthropist and his two young sons sat and

A full house at Wrigley paid tribute to Sosa's season while rooting for the Cubs to make the postseason.

chatted with Sosa. The father, Steve Ryan, a 40-year-old professional sports-memorabilia collector, had paid $10,000 for Sosa's 61st home run ball so that his sons could meet their idol when their dad gave the ball back to the man who had launched it. Fabian Perez Mercado, the fan who caught ball number 63—a grand slam in San Diego that tied Sosa with the St. Louis Cardinals' Mark McGwire in the home run race—gave that ball to Sosa too. Ball number 62, meanwhile, sat under court-ordered lock and key as a judge tried to sort out who it rightfully belonged to after one Chicagoan claimed another had stolen it from him in a mad scramble on Waveland Avenue.

In the Wrigley bleachers, things were more interesting. Two women lifted their shirts and tried their best to distract Dmitri Young, the Reds leftfielder. It didn't work. Of course, Young didn't have much to do on Friday, not with Sosa at bat, anyhow. He stood practically on the warning track, leaving all sorts of room for Sosa to try to bloop a single, but on this day Sosa never even got the ball out of the infield.

His best chance came in the fifth. The Cubs trailed 4–3 but had a man on second. Sosa came to bat and a thousand camera flashes went off in the bright afternoon. "I just need a base hit here," an old-school Bleacher Bum called out. "We're in the middle of a pennant race." The count was full when Reds starter Steve Parris threw a hanging curve. Sosa swung hugely and missed hugely. Strike three. For the day Sosa went 0 for 4, and the Cubs lost 6–4. His response to the game was beautifully sane. "I will go home, have a couple

The Sammy support system includes his mother Lucrecia (top), wife Sonia, and sons Michael (left) and Sammy Jr.

of glasses of wine with my wife and watch Mark hit a home run," he said. Which was what happened. While Sammy and Sonia sipped their wine, McGwire hit his 64th. On another channel the Mets lost to the Florida Marlins. The Cubs were still one game ahead.

There's no player in baseball who mentions his wife, mother, siblings and cousins in interviews more often than the 29-year-old Sosa does. His older brother Juan lives with Sammy during the season and serves as his unofficial batting coach. (Juan's main job is to remind

Sammy to keep his head back over his right foot to prevent overswinging.) Sammy's father, a highway worker, died of a brain aneurysm at age 42, when Sammy was seven, and it was Juan who encouraged Sammy to give up boxing in favor of baseball, encouraged Sammy to show up at various team tryouts in their hometown of San Pedro de Macoris and encouraged Sammy to shorten his looping swing.

Juan has another unofficial job: He's the family's representative-at-large to the city's Hispanic community. He plays in a softball league in Chicago and watches the Cubs' road games on TV at a Dominican social club on Chicago's West Side. The other night, when the Cubs were still in San Diego, Juan was at the club. It was a scene. A merengue band was rehearsing, a group of grown men drank beer and argued about whether President Clinton was going to heaven or hell and several young kids ran about. The game was on two television sets that could not be heard above the din. Then Slammin' Sammy came to bat, and everything went silent. Suddenly, four or five arms were draped around Juan's shoulders. Sammy whiffed, the arms disappeared, and Juan ducked his chin into his chest. The music and the arguments resumed.

Sonia watches most of the Cubs' games at home, even when the team is in Chicago. She's 24 and has four children, two girls followed by two boys, all under the age of six, and they need their mother, particularly the youngest, Michael. Sonia has a beautiful singing voice, and when Michael gets fussy she calms him by singing the

theme from *Titanic*. She was 17 and working as a dancer on a Dominican TV variety show when she met Sammy. He was 21 and playing minor league baseball. They were at a dance club in Santo Domingo when Sammy noticed her from a distance. He had a waiter bring her a note: "If you will do the honor of having one dance with me, it will be the start of a beautiful friendship." Sammy *Smooth*. "I looked at him and said, 'Oh, wow—what a man.'" Sonia says.

On Saturday, Sept. 19, Sosa was not the man. The breeze was blowing in at Wrigley, except when Sosa was at bat. He struck out swinging in his first three times up. For his finale, he grounded into a game-ending double play. The Reds won 7–2. In New York the Mets beat the Marlins 4–3. The wild-card race was even.

There are still at least three people involved with the Cubs who know firsthand the torture Chicago went through at the hands of the Mets in 1969. That was the year the Cubs had a 4½-game lead on Sept. 1 and finished the season trailing New York by eight games. Yosh Kawano, the equipment manager who has been with Chicago since '53, was around then. So was Billy Williams, the Cubs leftfielder in '69, now a Chicago coach. Those guys don't have much to say about '69. "The Mets were a team of destiny," Williams says. Then there's Ron Santo, the Cubs' third baseman in '69, today one of the team's radio announcers. Santo despises the Mets, has for 29 years. He has been passing down the history to the newly arrived in Chicago ever since. Some, like Sosa, care little about

Sosa belted No. 63—a grand slam—in San Diego (right), much to the delight of his Dominican supporters in Chicago, including his brother Juan (smiling).

history. He believes the 1998 Cubs are a team of destiny and harbors no animosity toward the Mets—or anyone else, for that matter.

The goodwill Sosa radiates was reflected back at him on Sunday, Sept. 20, Sammy Sosa Day at hallowed Wrigley. It may be true that poststrike baseball has a tendency to wallow in sentimentality, but this pregame ceremony was truly moving. For one thing, it was the final home game of the Cubs' season. Every seat was taken, everyone was paying attention. Michael Jordan was in the house, claiming graciously that Sosa's game is harder than his. Sosa's countryman Juan Marichal was there and a congratulatory letter from McGwire was read. Then came Ed Lynch,

the Cubs' shaggy general manager, wearing a rumpled sport coat, microphone in hand, his words reverberating off the outfield wall and upper deck, praising Sosa for having "the greatest season in the history of the Chicago Cubs." This may actually be true, although it could be argued that Hack Wilson had a better season for the Cubs in 1930 when he hit 56 homers and knocked in 190 runs. As Lynch spoke of Sosa's accomplishments, Ernie Banks, Mr. Cub himself, stood nearby waving a tiny Dominican flag.

When Sosa spoke, he thanked his God, his teammates, his fans, his adopted city, his family. He concluded by trotting out his favorite slogan, "Bezball been berry, berry good to me!" He then ran around the field, waving his cap. The Reds were applauding him, the grounds crew was applauding him, the ball hawks on Waveland were applauding him. The Bleacher Bums were bowing to him. Meanwhile, McGwire chose that moment to hit number 65, and Wrigley's primitive scoreboard showed that the Mets had taken an early lead over the Marlins.

Given where the Cubs were a year ago, it seems preposterous that they are even in a wild-card race. Chicago has a spectacular closer in Rod Beck, but getting to him is a daily adventure. The Cubs are where they are because of unexpected seasons from two players: Kerry Wood, the 21-year-old rookie righthander with a 13–6 record and a 3.40 ERA, and Sosa. There's nothing in Sosa's history to suggest that he would have an MVP-caliber season, much less put on one of the best hitting performances of the last 60 years. Before 1998 he had a .257 career batting average. He was batting .305 this year through Sept. 20. Entering this season, Sosa had hit a homer every 17.8 at bats. This year he had maintained a one-in-9.8 pace. Lynch, that disheveled genius, somehow saw this coming. Last year he signed Sosa to a four-year, $42 million deal.

Sosa made two significant changes this year. He dropped his hands at least six inches in his batting stance, which he says enabled him to get around on pitches faster. And he became far more patient at the plate, on first pitches in particular. He's also exceedingly confident. "When Sammy comes up after going 0 for 12, he feels he has the advantage, not the pitcher," says his manager, Jim Riggleman. Still, Sosa fights a tendency to be overeager. He tied McGwire with 63 homers on Sept. 16 and then in his next 17 at bats went hitless, striking out six times.

Unfortunately for the Cubs and the 40,000 fans at Wrigley participating in the festivities, five of those at bats came on Sammy Sosa Day, when Chicago lost its third straight to Cincinnati. That was not what the organizers of the celebration had in mind. Sosa's final at bat was in the ninth, with two outs and the Cubs trailing by four. The faithful in the rightfield bleachers, standing in a light rain, began their ritual, rhythmic chant, "SO-sa! SO-sa! SO-sa!" It was all short-lived. Sosa hit an infield pop-up, and the game was over. The Cubs had lost to the Reds 7–3, on a day when the Mets defeated the Marlins. On Friday, New York had trailed Chicago by a game. By Sunday's dusk the Cubs trailed by a game. On Friday McGwire and Sosa had been tied. Now McGwire was leading by two.

In losing, Sosa could not have been looser. After the game a reporter asked Sosa if Cubs fans had seen his final at bat for 1998 at Wrigley. Sosa understood the implication of the question, of course: Would the Cubs be playing October baseball for the first time since 1989? "What, am I going to die tomorrow?" he answered.

At the same session with reporters, a junior scribe, maybe ten years old, asked Sosa to identify his goal in life. "Go to heaven," he said, and then he laughed. He retreated to the Cubs' clubhouse, where he had a long beer with his brothers. He said he was a happy man, and he looked like a happy man, 0 for 17 and all. He looked like he was in heaven already.

83

The Greatest Season Ever

And so, as we all knew it would, the 1998 home run race came down to the final weekend, surging mightily to its tingling split-screen finish. Sosa pulled ahead briefly on Friday before a final McGwire explosion of five homers in his final three games settled the issue for good. Tom Verducci was there.

By Tom Verducci

When you sit down to tell the grandchildren the story, you might as well start out like this: Once upon a time.... For that is how all great fables begin. And when you do tell the tale of Mark McGwire and the great home run race of 1998, you should be careful to linger over each detail of the ending, smiling to yourself at how preposterous it is that every last bit of it is true.

At 8:39 p.m. CDT on the last Friday of the season, McGwire didn't even have the most home runs in the National League Central, let alone the most ever in one season. Just 45 minutes earlier in Houston, Sammy Sosa, the Chicago Cubs' redoubtable yang to McGwire's yin, had overtaken McGwire in a contest that resembled in its madness and score an NCAA basketball tournament game, 66–65. St. Louisans were aghast with fear. Even before the operator inside the Busch Stadium scoreboard replaced the 65 placard next to Sosa's name with a 66, McGwire, who was in the field at the time, knew what had happened. He could tell from the groans and murmurs of 48,159 fans. It was what anxiety sounds like.

McGwire himself was frazzled, looking like a downed power line in a storm. You could see the sparks, but the energy he worked up every day of the season to create what he called his "tunnel vision" of concentration had fried his mental circuits. He was darkly jovial as he walked to a press conference before that game last Friday. He took a gulp from his coffee cup and offered without prompting, "Seventy-two hours to go! It feels like a judge has sprung me. Seventy-two hours to freedom!"

Now McGwire was batting in the fifth inning, with a 1-and-2 count, against righthander Shayne Bennett of the Montreal Expos. The moment felt charged, the way it does when you're reading a great novel and the number of pages on the right side of the book gets thinner in your fingers. The excitement of the ending, still very much a mystery, was palpable.

The season's grand finale began when McGwire pounded an inside fastball from Bennett into the lower deck in leftfield, a home run that prompted "a great big sigh" when he

Exclamation point: With home run No. 70 in his last at bat, McGwire ended a glorious year gloriously.

84

The redoubtable Sosa took the home run lead for 45 minutes on Friday, but was unable to keep up with McGwire's torrid finish.

got back to the dugout, teammate Tom Lampkin said. In all, McGwire would blast five home runs with his last 19 swings. Most amazingly, his historic season that began on Opening Day with a grand slam ended with home runs on each of his final two swings, the last one a game-winning lightning bolt that left him with a number—70—as jaw-droppingly round as Babe Ruth's 60 seemed in 1927. "Obviously, it's a huge number," McGwire said on Sunday night. "I think the magnitude of the number won't be understood for a while. I mean,

it's unheard of for somebody to hit 70 home runs. So, I'm like in awe of myself right now."

Said Montreal manager Felipe Alou, "To hit 70 balls out in batting practice during a season isn't too easy for many people." Then, remembering his fellow Dominican, Alou said sadly, "I feel kind of empty for Sammy Sosa."

There was some consolation for Sosa in that he did, however briefly, join Ruth, Roger Maris and McGwire as holders of the home run record. But weep not for Sosa over the home run race. The first man ever to hit 66 could take solace from reaching the postseason for the first time. His streak of 1,247 games in the major leagues, ending with the Cubs' 5–3 victory on Monday night over the San Francisco Giants in a one-game playoff for the National League wild-card berth, was the longest active postseasonless streak of any big leaguer except Dave Martinez of the Tampa Bay Devil Rays.

In his last 40 games McGwire smashed 23 home runs, such a ridiculous sum that it would have led the Cardinals in 22 of the previous 32 seasons. The last three games in particular put him not just in the company of Ruth, who hit 17 homers in September 1927, and Ted Williams, whose six hits in eight at bats on the final day of the 1941 season gave him a .406 average. No, McGwire also joined Michael Jordan, Secretariat and Aesop among the greatest finishers of all time. "I can't believe I did it," he told reporters at his final postgame press conference. "Can you? It's absolutely amazing. It blows me away."

Believe. The chase by McGwire and Sosa of Maris's record 61 home runs—and then of each other—spread the religion of baseball. Cardinals and Cubs games had the feel of revival meetings. No other teams in baseball averaged more fans on the road. And baseball, a setup line to cruel jokes during and after the 1994–95 strike, regained its honor. Hardly anyone complained about the length of games or nitpicked about Nielsen ratings. Hallelujah!

MARK MCGWIRE, said a sign at Busch Stadium on Sunday, THE BEST THERE EVER WAS. The same could be said for the 1998 season. Williams's run at .400 and Joe DiMaggio's 56-game hitting streak made '41 special. The races in '08 were so tight that four teams came within 1½ games

of a pennant. But no other year was so full of seismic events that shook even casual and never-before fans into paying attention. And St. Louis was the epicenter.

"As far as I'm concerned, it's the best season ever," says Alou, who has spent 40 years in baseball. "The game has emerged from the grave with thunder. You don't hear about the strike anymore. Sometimes, something has to almost die, like baseball did, for the miracle to take place. The average fan has more faith in the game now."

Baseball was a cool topic at the water cooler again, and nothing stirred the conversation as the home run race did. McGwire or Sosa? Who do you like? How many will they hit? Even McGwire played the game. On Sept. 21, with 65 dingers on the eve of his last six games, he asked his close friend Ali Dickson to guess the final number and keep it a secret. She wrote it down on a piece of paper and stashed it away.

Heads of state paid attention and homage. The President of the United States congratulated McGwire upon home run number 62. The President of the Czech Republic invoked McGwire's and Sosa's names during his visit to Washington. The Prime Minister of Japan sent Big Mac a letter. The music industry plugged in, with Bruce Springsteen, Steven Tyler, Bruce Hornsby and the Dixie Chicks among those requesting audiences with McGwire in September.

The sports world felt like the 1950s again, with a locked-out NBA suddenly irrelevant and

87

an overshadowed NFL pushed to the inside pages of sports sections. The definitive moment of reclamation for baseball came on Sunday, when the crowd at the St. Louis Rams–Arizona Cardinals football game, being played a few blocks from Busch Stadium, made so much noise on a third-and-nine play that the disoriented Rams took an illegal motion penalty. The reason for the distraction? McGwire had just hit his 69th.

The home run race left its imprint everywhere, including on the scoreboards of Senior PGA events, where golfer Hugh Baiocchi looked up to see SOSA 61 on the leader board in late September and wondered, Who the devil is Sosa? He must have come out of the pack.

At another Senior event, outside St. Louis last Saturday, golfer Larry Nelson heard a roar go up as a competitor's shot hit the fringe of the 14th green and rolled off. Wow, this is a tough crowd, Nelson thought. They must really hate this guy. Then he learned the fans were reacting to McGwire's 67th. Big Mac's home runs traveled—and well beyond the mountainous total of 29,598 accumulated feet his 70 blasts were measured at.

"There was only one thing we wanted from him," said Marilyn Chapman, the wife of the 48-year-old man who caught and returned McGwire's 66th home run ball. "That was a hug. And it was a good hug."

McGwire and Sosa restored baseball's importance as the last great civil game, a worthy and welcome thing at a time when politics and television have coagulated into such an unseemly mess that Peter Jennings and Jerry Springer cover similar ground. Of course, McGwire's manners belied the ferocity with which he set the record. He had a slugging percentage of .752—only Ruth, Lou Gehrig and Rogers Hornsby have done better—while whacking one out of every five balls he put into play out of the park. "You try to think of more adjectives, but you run out of them," Tom Lampkin said on Saturday. "You run out of words in the thesaurus. The one word that keeps popping up is unbelievable. It's truly unbelievable."

McGwire lost more balls against the Expos than a weekend duffer at Sawgrass. On Friday, Saturday and Sunday he belted homers against Montreal's Bennett, Dustin Hermanson, Kirk Bullinger, Mike Thurman and Carl Pavano, none of whom was older than 28 or had pitched in the big leagues before 1997. The one against Bullinger on Saturday was clocked at 111 mph going out. "It was a laser going past me," Bullinger said afterward. "By the time I turned around, it was landing in the bleachers."

Thurman gave up home run number 69 in the third inning on Sunday, a majestic rainbow into the lower deck in left. In the fifth, with a base open and orders from Alou against giving McGwire anything to hit, Thurman walked Big Mac on four pitches. Then, in the seventh with two runners on, two outs and the score tied 3–3, Alou said nothing to Pavano. "I left it up to God and history," Alou said later. "I didn't want to tamper with history."

With his unassailable 70 home runs safely in the record books, McGwire took one last bow as a packed house saluted 1998's biggest hero.

Said Pavano, "I was going right after him. He went right after me." McGwire sent Pavano's 96-mph fastball screaming over the leftfield wall with such pace that it may as well have been marked TITLEIST as RAWLINGS.

Now it was safe for Dickson to reveal to McGwire on their plane ride home to California what number she had written down at the start of the week: 71. "And really, if you count the home run in Milwaukee, that's what it was," she said, recalling the fan-interference call by umpire Bob Davidson on Sept. 20, which turned a possible home run into a double.

Not DiMaggio's streak or any pennant race held us spellbound for so long as did the great home run race. Excluding the All-Star break, Sosa or McGwire homered on more days (90) than they didn't (88). The final six weeks were especially frantic, like a movie chase scene, with one or both of them hitting a home run on 26 of the last 40 days—never letting more than two days pass without one.

The best there ever was. This is how the story ends. It made believers of us all.

Postscript

By Merrell Noden

Will McGwire watch as many of his moon shots leave the yard in 1999 as in '98?

Now that the delirium has finally passed and we slump back amazed by all those incomprehensible numbers, it is time to find some perspective. Perspective, after all, was as hard to come by in the waning days of the baseball season as bleacher seats at Wrigley on those rare, magical days when McGwire and Sosa were both in town.

Any way you look at the numbers, this was an extraordinary year for power hitting. The 50-homer season, a benchmark reached only three times in the quarter century from 1965 through 1990 and by no more than two players in any season past, was topped by four men this year: It was annihilated by Mark McGwire (70) and Sammy Sosa (66), beaten by Ken Griffey Jr. (56), and equaled by Greg Vaughn, who jumped from 18 in 1997 to 50 in 1998. What's more, nine other players, led by Albert Belle (49), hit 40 or more homers. That's four shy of the alltime record of 17 set in 1996, the year with the greatest total home run output, but it's still breathtaking.

Even after Griffey fell hopelessly behind McGwire and Sosa in August, others stepped in to spread home run fever around the American League. Albert Belle of the Chicago White Sox went on a tear in July, hitting 16 homers, and Manny Ramirez of the Cleveland Indians homered five times in consecutive games in mid-September to tie the major league record. And in the tall tale department, a journeyman outfielder named Shane Spencer, who had spent eight seasons in the minors, was brought up by the Yankees on Aug. 31 and promptly went ballistic, ripping 10 home runs in 67 at bats, including three grand slams in 10 days. Cynics will no doubt chalk those prodigious numbers up to the effects of expansion, to the dilution of the pitching talent pool that almost inevitably boosts great hitters, making them sharks feeding on minnows.

Can we expect another home run bonanza next year? That's a tough question. There is no reason to assume that Griffey, who has hit 56 in each of the last two seasons, can't hit more. Sosa's chances may be slimmer: If anonymity helped him this year, it's a boost he won't get again. In Sosa's favor are the "intangibles," which baseball fans love to debate even as we pay obeisance to cold statistics: Was Sosa hurt by playing for a contender, and how much? McGwire's Cardinals, after all, were out of it when the home run race heated up in mid-August; he could swing from the heels every time he came to bat. Sosa, on the other hand, had to worry about making contact, moving runners.

That brings us to McGwire, who is now working on an unprecedented streak of three straight 50-plus seasons. Even Ruth never did that. In assessing whether McGwire can hit 70 again, it's tempting to recall all the times he was denied a chance to homer: He was walked 162 times this year, a National League record and second alltime to Ruth's 170. Sosa, by contrast, had just 73. Taking McGwire's 1998 homer rate of one every 7.3 at bats and extrapolating over his 89 fewer at bats than Sosa, we award him 12 more theoretical homers. But that's theory: Is it really going to change? Or will this season's display of power make rival pitchers even more reluctant to pitch to him?

And what of Aaron's career total of 755 home runs? McGwire finished this season 20th on the career home run list, with 457. That leaves him almost 300 behind Aaron's 755. McGwire, who turned 35 on Oct. 1, has said he plans to play until he's 40 and then retire to coach. Merely to sneak by Aaron will require his averaging 60 homers a year until then. That's hard to imagine, even if he stays healthy, a tough proposition for a player who missed much of the 1993 and '94 seasons with a stress fracture of the left heel requiring surgery and who this year suffered with back problems. In those two injury-plagued seasons McGwire hit just 18 home runs total; replace those with average McGwire seasons of 44 homers—for a boost of 70 in all—and he might have a real shot at Aaron. As it stands, his chances are slim at best. Of course, should he change his plans and choose to play past 40, we may have to revise our estimate.

The man with the best chance by far is Griffey, whose 56 homers this year pushed him past the 350 mark faster than anyone in baseball history. At age 28, he is nearly halfway there.

But what of the emotional toll taken by the pursuit of any great record? McGwire is by all accounts a fairly unassuming guy who at times looked to be enduring this season more than enjoying it. There is a time-honored baseball law that forbids a player to elevate himself over his team, and McGwire clearly did not enjoy having to break it day after day.

"If you were able to take an X-ray of my insides over the past two weeks, I'd hate to have seen it," McGwire later admitted in a first person piece he wrote with SI's Tom Verducci. "My insides were churning."

And it looked that way. As McGwire himself reminded us again and again, it is the mental side of the chase that is hardest. Knowing what he now knows, will he ever subject himself to that sort of torment again?

Home Run Roster

MARK McGWIRE

No.	Date	Game	Team	Pitcher	Dist	Inning	Outs	Count	Men On
1	Mar 31	1	LA	Ramon Martinez (R)	364	5	2	1-0	3
2	Apr 2	2	LA	Frank Lankford (R)	368	12	2	0-1	2
3	Apr 3	3	SD	Mark Langston (L)	364	5	0	3-2	1
4	Apr 4	4	SD	Don Wengert (R)	419	6	0	2-1	2
5	Apr 14	13	Ariz	Jeff Suppan (R)	424	3	1	1-2	1
6	Apr 14	13	Ariz	Jeff Suppan (R)	347	5	2	1-1	0
7	Apr 14	13	Ariz	Barry Manuel (R)	462	8	0	2-0	1
8	Apr 17	16	Phil	Matt Whiteside (R)	419	4	2	2-2	1
9	Apr 21	19	at Mtl	Trey Moore (L)	437	3	2	0-0	1
10	Apr 25	23	at Phil	Jerry Spradlin (R)	419	7	2	1-2	1
11	Apr 30	27	at Chi (N)	Marc Pisciotta (R)	371	8	1	2-1	1
12	May 1	28	at Chi (N)	Rod Beck (R)	362	9	2	1-2	1
13	May 8	34	at NY (N)	Rick Reed (R)	358	3	1	0-2	1
14	May 12	36	Mil	Paul Wagner (R)	527	5	0	1-2	2
15	May 14	38	Atl	Kevin Millwood (R)	361	4	0	1-1	0
16	May 16	40	Fla	Livan Hernandez (R)	545	4	0	1-0	0
17	May 18	42	Fla	Jesus Sanchez (L)	478	4	0	2-0	0
18	May 19	43	at Phil	Tyler Green (R)	440	3	1	2-0	1
19	May 19	43	at Phil	Tyler Green (R)	471	5	0	0-2	1
20	May 19	43	at Phil	Wayne Gomes (R)	451	8	0	0-0	1
21	May 22	46	SF	Mark Gardner (R)	425	6	1	1-1	1
22	May 23	47	SF	Rich Rodriguez (L)	366	4	1	1-0	0
23	May 23	47	SF	John Johnstone (R)	477	5	1	2-2	2
24	May 24	48	SF	Robb Nen (R)	397	12	2	2-2	1
25	May 25	49	Col	John Thomson (R)	433	1	2	2-2	0
26	May 29	52	at SD	Dan Miceli (R)	388	9	1	0-1	1
27	May 30	53	at SD	Andy Ashby (R)	423	1	2	0-1	0
28	June 5	59	SF	Orel Hershiser (R)	409	1	1	1-2	1
29	June 8	62	at Chi (A)	Jason Bere (R)	356	4	0	0-0	1
30	June 10	64	at Chi (A)	Jim Parque (L)	409	3	1	1-0	2
31	June 12	65	at Ariz	Andy Benes (R)	438	3	1	1-0	3
32	June 17	69	at Hou	Jose Lima (R)	347	3	2	1-2	0
33	June 18	70	at Hou	Shane Reynolds (R)	449	5	0	1-1	0
34	June 24	76	at Clev	Jaret Wright (R)	433	4	1	1-1	0

No.	Date	Game	Team	Pitcher	Dist	Inning	Outs	Count	Men On
35	June 25	77	at Clev	Dave Burba (R)	461	1	2	2-2	0
36	June 27	79	at Minn	Mike Trombley (R)	431	7	2	2-2	1
37	June 30	81	KC	Glendon Rusch (L)	472	7	0	0-1	0
38	July 11	89	Hou	Billy Wagner (L)	485	11	1	0-2	1
39	July 12	90	Hou	Sean Bergman (R)	405	1	2	0-0	0
40	July 12	90	Hou	Scott Elarton (R)	415	7	0	2-1	0
41	July 17	95	LA	Brian Bohanon (L)	511	1	2	0-0	0
42	July 17	95	LA	Antonio Osuna (R)	425	8	1	1-0	0
43	July 20	98	at SD	Brian Boehringer (R)	458	5	0	2 1	1
44	July 26	104	at Col	John Thomson (R)	452	4	2	0-0	0
45	July 28	105	Mil	Mike Myers (L)	408	8	1	2-2	0
46	Aug 8	115	Chi (N)	Mark Clark (R)	374	4	0	2-1	0
47	Aug 11	118	NY (N)	Bobby Jones (R)	464	4	0	1-0	0
48	Aug 19	124	at Chi (N)	Matt Karchner (R)	430	8	1	3-1	0
49	Aug 19	124	at Chi (N)	Terry Mulholland (L)	402	10	1	2-0	0
50	Aug 20	125	at NY (N)	Willie Blair (R)	369	7	0	2-1	0
51	Aug 20	126	at NY (N)	Rick Reed (R)	385	1	2	3-2	0
52	Aug 22	129	at Pitt	Francisco Cordova (R)	477	1	2	0-2	0
53	Aug 23	130	at Pitt	Ricardo Rincon (L)	393	8	2	2-2	0
54	Aug 26	133	Fla	Justin Speier (R)	509	8	0	0-1	1
55	Aug 30	137	Atl	Dennis Martinez (R)	501	7	0	1-0	2
56	Sept 1	139	at Fla	Livan Hernandez (R)	450	7	0	1-1	0
57	Sept 1	139	at Fla	Donn Pall (R)	472	9	1	0-0	0
58	Sept 2	140	at Fla	Brian Edmondson (R)	497	7	2	2-1	1
59	Sept 2	140	at Fla	Robby Stanifer (R)	458	8	2	0-0	1
60	Sept 5	142	Cin	Dennis Reyes (L)	381	1	1	2-0	1
61	Sept 7	144	Chi (N)	Mike Morgan (R)	430	1	2	1-1	0
62	Sept 8	145	Chi (N)	Steve Trachsel (R)	341	4	2	0-0	0
63	Sept 15	152	Pitt	Jason Christiansen (L)	385	9	0	1-0	0
64	Sept 18	155	at Mil	Rafael Roque (L)	417	4	0	3-1	1
65	Sept 20	157	at Mil	Scott Karl (L)	423	1	1	2-1	1
66	Sept 25	161	Mtl	Shayne Bennett (R)	379	5	2	1-2	1
67	Sept 26	162	Mtl	Dustin Hermanson (R)	403	4	1	0-0	0
68	Sept 26	162	Mtl	Kirk Bullinger (R)	435	7	2	1-1	1
69	Sept 27	163	Mtl	Mike Thurman (R)	377	3	2	2-2	0
70	Sept 27	163	Mtl	Carl Pavano (R)	370	7	2	2-2	2

Home Run Roster

SAMMY SOSA

No.	Date	Game	Team	Pitcher	Dist	Inning	Outs	Count	Men On
1	Apr 4	5	Mtl	Marc Valdes (R)	371	3	2	2-1	0
2	Apr 11	11	at Mtl	Anthony Telford (R)	350	7	1	1-2	0
3	Apr 15	14	at NY (N)	Dennis Cook (L)	430	8	2	3-2	0
4	Apr 23	21	SD	Dan Miceli (R)	420	9	0	0-1	0
5	Apr 24	22	at LA	Ismael Valdes (R)	430	1	2	3-1	0
6	Apr 27	25	at SD	Joey Hamilton (R)	434	1	1	0-1	1
7	May 3	30	StL	Cliff Politte (R)	370	1	2	2-1	0
8	May 16	42	at Cin	Scott Sullivan (R)	420	3	1	2-1	2
9	May 22	47	at Atl	Greg Maddux (R)	440	1	2	2-2	0
10	May 25	50	at Atl	Kevin Millwood (R)	410	4	0	2-2	0
11	May 25	50	at Atl	Mike Cather (R)	420	8	2	0-1	2
12	May 27	51	Phil	Darrin Winston (L)	460	8	0	1-2	0
13	May 27	51	Phil	Wayne Gomes (R)	400	9	2	0-0	1
14	June 1	56	Fla	Ryan Dempster (R)	430	1	1	1-0	1
15	June 1	56	Fla	Oscar Henriquez (R)	410	8	2	1-0	2
16	June 3	58	Fla	Livan Hernandez (R)	370	5	0	1-0	1
17	June 5	59	Chi (A)	Jim Parque (L)	370	5	0	1-2	1
18	June 6	60	Chi (A)	Carlos Castillo (R)	410	7	2	2-2	0
19	June 7	61	Chi (A)	James Baldwin (R)	380	5	1	3-2	2
20	June 8	62	at Minn	LaTroy Hawkins (R)	340	3	1	0-2	0
21	June 13	66	at Phil	Mark Portugal (R)	350	6	0	0-1	1
22	June 15	68	Mil	Cal Eldred (R)	420	1	2	1-0	0
23	June 15	68	Mil	Cal Eldred (R)	410	3	1	2-1	0
24	June 15	68	Mil	Cal Eldred (R)	415	7	2	2-1	0
25	June 17	70	Mil	Bronswell Patrick (R)	430	4	0	2-2	0
26	June 19	72	Phil	Carlton Loewer (R)	380	1	2	2-2	0
27	June 19	72	Phil	Carlton Loewer (R)	380	5	1	1-0	1
28	June 20	73	Phil	Matt Beech (L)	366	3	2	3-2	1
29	June 20	73	Phil	Toby Borland (R)	500	6	1	2-0	2
30	June 21	74	Phil	Tyler Green (R)	380	4	2	2-2	0
31	June 24	77	at Det	Seth Greisinger (R)	390	1	1	0-2	0
32	June 25	78	at Det	Brian Moehler (R)	400	7	0	1-0	0

No.	Date	Game	Team	Pitcher	Dist	Inning	Outs	Count	Men On
33	June 30	82	Ariz	Alan Embree (L)	364	8	1	3-2	0
34	July 9	88	at Mil	Jeff Juden (R)	430	2	2	0-2	1
35	July 10	89	at Mil	Scott Karl (L)	450	2	0	1-0	0
36	July 17	95	at Fla	Kirt Ojala (L)	440	6	2	2-1	1
37	July 22	100	Mtl	Miguel Batista (R)	365	8	2	1-0	2
38	July 26	105	NY (N)	Rick Reed (R)	420	6	1	2-2	1
39	July 27	106	at Ariz	Willie Blair (R)	350	6	2	1-1	1
40	July 27	106	at Ariz	Alan Embree (L)	420	8	0	0-0	3
41	July 28	107	at Ariz	Bob Wolcott (R)	400	5	1	3-1	3
42	July 31	110	Col	Jamey Wright (R)	380	1	2	3-2	0
43	Aug 5	115	Ariz	Andy Benes (R)	380	3	2	3-2	1
44	Aug 8	117	at StL	Rich Croushore (R)	400	9	0	1-0	1
45	Aug 10	119	at SF	Russ Ortiz (R)	370	5	2	3-1	0
46	Aug 10	119	at SF	Chris Brock (R)	420	7	2	2-1	0
47	Aug 16	124	at Hou	Sean Bergman (R)	360	4	1	0-1	0
48	Aug 19	126	StL	Kent Bottenfield (R)	368	5	2	0-0	1
49	Aug 21	128	SF	Orel Hershiser (R)	430	5	1	3-2	1
50	Aug 23	130	Hou	Jose Lima (R)	433	5	2	3-2	0
51	Aug 23	130	Hou	Jose Lima (R)	388	8	0	1-0	0
52	Aug 26	133	at Cinn	Brett Tomko (R)	440	3	2	1-1	0
53	Aug 28	135	at Col	John Thomson (R)	414	1	2	1-2	0
54	Aug 30	137	at Col	Darryl Kile (R)	482	1	1	1-2	1
55	Aug 31	138	Cinn	Brett Tomko (R)	364	3	2	0-1	1
56	Sept 2	140	Cinn	Jason Bere (R)	370	6	0	0-1	0
57	Sept 4	141	at Pitt	Jason Schmidt (R)	400	1	2	2-0	0
58	Sept 5	142	at Pitt	Sean Lawrence (L)	405	6	0	3-1	0
59	Sept 11	148	Mil	Bill Pulsipher (L)	433	5	1	0-1	0
60	Sept 12	149	Mil	Valerio De Los Santos (L)	390	7	1	3-2	2
61	Sept 13	150	Mil	Bronswell Patrick (R)	480	5	0	0-1	1
62	Sept 13	150	Mil	Eric Plunk (R)	480	9	1	2-1	0
63	Sept 16	153	at SD	Brian Boehringer (R)	434	8	2	1-0	3
64	Sept 23	159	at Mil	Rafael Roque (L)	344	5	1	1-0	0
65	Sept 23	159	at Mil	Rodney Henderson (R)	410	6	2	2-2	0
66	Sept 25	160	at Hou	Jose Lima (R)	462	4	0	0-1	0

Home Run Breakdown

BY DAY OF THE WEEK

	McGwire	Sosa
Monday	5	14
Tuesday	16	2
Wednesday	8	14
Thursday	7	3
Friday	11	13
Saturday	13	10
Sunday	10	10

BY LOCATION

	McGwire	Sosa
Home	38	35
Road	32	31
Artificial Turf	10	9
Grass	60	57

BY TYPE OF PITCHER

	McGwire	Sosa
Starters	39	44
Relievers	31	22
Righties	55	54
Lefties	15	12

BY INNING

	McGwire	Sosa
First	11	12
Second	0	2
Third	8	8
Fourth	13	5
Fifth	9	12
Sixth	2	8
Seventh	10	6
Eighth	9	9
Ninth	4	4
Extra innings	4	0

BY SPOT IN BATTING ORDER (AB/HR)

	McGwire	Sosa
First	*2/1	0/0
Third	506/69	487/49
Fourth	0/0	156/17
Ninth	*1/0	0/0

*At bats were as a pinch hitter

BY NUMBER OF OUTS

	McGwire	Sosa
None out	21	16
One out	22	20
Two outs	27	30

BY DIRECTION

	McGwire	Sosa
Left	37	12
Left-center	17	22
Center	13	10
Right-center	3	11
Right	0	11

BY COUNT

	McGwire	Sosa
0-0	11	3
0-1	5	10
0-2	4	3
1-0	9	12
1-1	9	2
1-2	7	5
2-0	5	2
2-1	8	8
2-2	8	8
3-0	0	0
3-1	2	4
3-2	2	9

BY MEN ON BASE

	McGwire	Sosa
Bases empty	33	37
Runner on 1st	17	16
Runner on 2nd	6	3
Runner on 3rd	5	0
Runners on 1st/2nd	4	4
Runners on 1st/3rd	2	2
Runners on 2nd/3rd	1	1
Bases loaded	2	3

BY DISTANCE (IN FEET)

	McGwire	Sosa
300-349	3	2
350-399	20	24
400-449	26	34
450-499	16	5
500 and over	5	1
Average	423	405

BY MONTH

	McGwire	Sosa
March/Apr	11	6
May	16	7
June	10	20
July	8	9
August	10	13
September	15	11

Photo Credits

COVER: McGwire, V.J. Lovero; Sosa, Stephen Green.

BACK COVER: John Biever.

FRONT MATTER: Half-title page, V.J. Lovero; Title page, Stephen Green.

INTRODUCTION: 6, David E. Klutho; 8, Stephen Green.

CHASING HISTORY
10–11, Stephen Green; 13, V.J. Lovero; 14, V.J. Lovero; 17, Brad Mangin; 19, Stephen Green; 21, the McGwire family; 23, John Biever; 24 left, Chuck Solomon; right, Stephen Green; 26, Stephen Green; 28, Jonathan Daniel; 30 top left, John Biever; top right, V.J. Lovero; bottom, Ronald C. Modra; 32 top, Stephen Green; bottom, V.J. Lovero; 35, John Biever.

HISTORY IN SIGHT
36–37, V.J. Lovero; 39 left, Stephen Green; right, Stephen Green; 41, John Biever; 42, John Biever; 43, Chuck Solomon; 45, V.J. Lovero; 46, V.J. Lovero; 49 top and bottom, V.J. Lovero; 50, David E. Klutho; 53, John Biever; 54 left, Stephen Green; right, Simon Bruty; 56, V.J. Lovero; 58, David E. Klutho; 59, John Biever; 60, John Biever; 62, Tim Broekema/Allsport; 65, Stephen Green; 67, Walter Iooss Jr.; 68, V.J. Lovero; 71, V.J. Lovero; 72, illustration, Victor Juhasz; 74, illustration, Victor Juhasz; 77, illustration, Victor Juhasz; 79, John Iacono; 80 top, Victor Baldizon; bottom, Todd Buchanan; 82 left, Todd Rosenberg; right, V.J. Lovero; 85, V.J. Lovero; 86, Vincent La Foret/Allsport; 89, Walter Iooss Jr.; 90, David Gonzales/Clarkson and Associates.